Essentials of Intellectual Disability Assessment and Identification

Essentials of **Psychological Assessment** Series

Everything you need to know to administer, score, and interpret the major psychological tests

I'd like to order the following *Essentials of Psychological Assessment:*

❏ WAIS®-IV Assessment, Second
Edition (w/CD-ROM)
978-1-118-27188-9 • $50.00

❏ WJ® IV Tests of Achievement
978-1-118-79915-4 • $40.00

❏ Cross-Battery Assessment,
Third Edition (w/CD-ROM)
978-0-470-62195-0 • $50.00

❏ Executive Functions Assessment
(w/CD-ROM)
978-0-470-42202-1 • $50.00

❏ WPPSI™-IV Assessment
(w/CD-ROM)
978-1-11838062-8 • $50.00

❏ Specific Learning Disability
Identification
978-0-470-58760-7 • $40.00

❏ IDEA for Assessment Professionals
(w/CD-ROM)
978-0-470-87392-2 • $50.00

❏ Dyslexia Assessment
and Intervention
978-0-470-92760-1 • $40.00

❏ Autism Spectrum Disorders
Evaluation and Assessment
978-0-470-62194-3 • $40.00

❏ Planning, Selecting, and Tailoring
Interventions for Unique Learners
(w/CD-ROM)
978-1-118-36821-3 • $50.00

❏ Processing Assessment,
Second Edition (w/CD-ROM)
978-1-118-36820-6 • $50.00

❏ School Neuropsychological
Assessment, Second Edition
(w/CD-ROM)
978-1-118-17584-2 • $50.00

❏ Gifted Assessment
978-1-118-58920-5 • $40.00

❏ Working Memory Assessment
and Intervention
978-1-118-63813-2 • $50.00

❏ Assessing, Preventing, and
Overcoming Reading Difficulties
978-1-118-84524-0 • $50.00

❏ Evidence-Based
Academic Interventions
978-0-470-20632-4 • $40.00

❏ Nonverbal Assessment
978-0-471-38318-5 • $40.00

❏ PAI® Assessment
978-0-471-08463-1 • $40.00

❏ CAS Assessment
978-0-471-29015-5 • $40.00

❏ MMPI®-2 Assessment,
Second Edition
978-0-470-92323-8 • $40.00

❏ Myers-Briggs Type Indicator®
Assessment, Second Edition
978-0-470-34390-6 • $40.00

❏ Rorschach® Assessment
978-0-471-33146-9 • $40.00

❏ Millon™ Inventories Assessment,
Third Edition
978-0-470-16862-2 • $40.00

❏ TAT and Other Storytelling
Assessments, Second Edition
978-0-470-28192-5 • $40.00

❏ MMPI-A™ Assessment
978-0-471-39815-8 • $40.00

❏ NEPSY®-II Assessment
978-0-470-43691-2 • $40.00

❏ Neuropsychological Assessment,
Second Edition
978-0-470-43747-6 • $40.00

❏ Essentials of WJ IV®
Cognitive Abilities Assessment
978-1-119-16336-7 • $50.00

❏ WRAML2 and TOMAL-2 Assessment
978-0-470-17911-6 • $40.00

❏ WMS®-IV Assessment
978-0-470-62196-7 • $40.00

❏ Behavioral Assessment
978-0-471-35367-6 • $40.00

❏ Forensic Psychological
Assessment, Second Edition
978-0-470-55168-4 • $40.00

❏ Intellectual Disability Assessment
and Identification
978-1-118-87509-4 • $40.00

❏ Bayley Scales of Infant
Development II Assessment
978-0-471-32651-9 • $40.00

❏ Career Interest Assessment
978-0-471-35365-2 • $40.00

❏ 16PF® Assessment
978-0-471-23424-1 • $40.00

❏ Assessment Report Writing
978-0-471-39487-7 • $40.00

❏ Stanford-Binet Intelligence Scales
(SB5) Assessment
978-0-471-22404-4 • $40.00

❏ WISC®-IV Assessment,
Second Edition (w/CD-ROM)
978-0-470-18915-3 • $50.00

❏ KABC-II Assessment
978-0-471-66733-9 • $40.00

❏ WIAT®-III and KTEA-II Assessment
(w/CD-ROM)
978-0-470-55169-1 • $50.00

❏ Cognitive Assessment with
KAIT & Other Kaufman Measures
978-0-471-38317-8 • $40.00

❏ Assessment with Brief
Intelligence Tests
978-0-471-26412-5 • $40.00

❏ Creativity Assessment
978-0-470-13742-0 • $40.00

❏ WNV™ Assessment
978-0-470-28467-4 • $40.00

❏ DAS-II® Assessment (w/CD-ROM)
978-0-470-22520-2 • $50.00

❏ Conners Behavior Assessments™
978-0-470-34633-4 • $40.00

❏ Temperament Assessment
978-0-470-44447-4 • $40.00

❏ Response to Intervention
978-0-470-56663-3 • $40.00

❏ ADHD Assessment
for Children and Adolescents
978-1-118-11270-0 • $40.00

Please complete the order form on the back. • To order by phone, call toll free 1-877-762-2974
To order online: www.wiley.com/essentials • To order by mail: refer to order form on next page

WILEY

Essentials

of **Psychological Assessment** Series

ORDER FORM

Please send this order form with your payment (credit card or check) to:
Wiley, Attn: Customer Care, 10475 Crosspoint Blvd., Indianapolis, IN 46256

QUANTITY	TITLE	ISBN	PRICE
_____	_____	_____	_____
_____	_____	_____	_____
_____	_____	_____	_____
_____	_____	_____	_____
_____	_____	_____	_____

Shipping Charges:	Surface	2-Day	1-Day
First item	$5.00	$10.50	$17.50
Each additional item	$3.00	$3.00	$4.00

For orders greater than 15 items,
please contact Customer Care at 1-877-762-2974.

ORDER AMOUNT _____

SHIPPING CHARGES _____

SALES TAX _____

TOTAL ENCLOSED _____

NAME_____

AFFILIATION_____

ADDRESS_____

CITY/STATE/ZIP_____

TELEPHONE_____

EMAIL_____

❑ Please add me to your e-mailing list

PAYMENT METHOD:

❑ Check/Money Order   ❑ Visa   ❑ Mastercard   ❑ AmEx

Card Number _____ Exp. Date _____

Cardholder Name (Please print) _____

Signature _____

Make checks payable to **John Wiley & Sons.** Credit card orders invalid if not signed.
All orders subject to credit approval. • Prices subject to change.

To order by phone, call toll free 1-877-762-2974
To order online: www.wiley.com/essentials

WILEY

Essentials of Psychological Assessment Series
Series Editors, Alan S. Kaufman and Nadeen L. Kaufman

Essentials

of Intellectual Disability Assessment and Identification

Alan W. Brue
Linda Wilmshurst

WILEY

Library of Congress Cataloging-in-Publication Data

Names: Brue, Alan W., author. | Wilmshurst, Linda, author.
Title: Essentials of intellectual disability assessment and identification /
   Alan W. Brue, Linda Wilmshurst.
Description: Hoboken, New Jersey : John Wiley & Sons, Inc., [2016] | Series:
   Essentials of psychological assessment | Includes index.
Identifiers: LCCN 2015051194| ISBN 9781118875094 (paperback) | ISBN 9781118875643 (ePDF)
   ISBN 9781118875537 (epub)
Subjects: LCSH: Mental retardation. | Developmental disabilities. |
   Intelligence tests. | Educational tests and measurements. | BISAC:
   PSYCHOLOGY / Assessment, Testing & Measurement.
Classification: LCC RC570 .B78 2016 | DDC 362.3—dc23 LC record available at
   http://lccn.loc.gov/2015051194

CONTENTS

This book is dedicated to the memory of my mentor and friend, Dr. Thomas Oakland, who has been and continues to be an inspiration to many around the world.

—Alan W. Brue

SERIES PREFACE

I n the *Essentials of Psychological Assessment* series, we have attempted to provide the reader with books that will deliver key practical information in the most efficient and accessible style. Many books in the series feature specific instruments in a variety of domains, such as cognition, personality, education, and neuropsychology. Other books, like *Essentials of Intellectual Disability Assessment and Identification*, focus on crucial topics for professionals who are involved in any way with assessment—topics such as specific reading disabilities, evidence-based interventions, and ADHD assessment. For the experienced professional, books in the series offer a concise yet thorough review of a test instrument or a specific area of expertise, including numerous tips for best practices. Students can turn to series books for a clear and concise overview of the important assessment tools and of key topics in which they must become proficient to practice skillfully, efficiently, and ethically in their chosen fields.

Wherever feasible, visual cues highlighting key points are utilized alongside systematic, step-by-step guidelines. Chapters are focused and succinct. Topics are organized for an easy understanding of the essential material related to a particular test or topic. Theory and research are continually woven into the fabric of each book, but the aim always is to enhance the practical application of the material rather than to sidetrack or overwhelm readers. With this series, we aim to challenge and assist readers interested in psychological assessment to aspire to the highest level of competency by arming them with the tools they need for knowledgeable, informed practice. We have long been advocates of "intelligent" testing—the notion that numbers are meaningless unless they are brought to life by the clinical acumen and expertise of examiners. Assessment must be used to make a difference in the child's or adult's life, or why bother to test? All books in the series—whether devoted to specific tests or general topics—are consistent with this credo. We want this series to help our readers, novice and veteran alike, to benefit from the intelligent assessment approaches of the authors of each book.

We are delighted to include *Essentials of Intellectual Disability Assessment and Identification* in our series. This book offers a concise overview of the nature of an intellectual disability and adaptive skills functioning in children, adolescents, and adults. Providing an in-depth look at intellectual disability assessment and identification, the authors discuss the history of intellectual disability, its causes, comorbid disorders, diagnostic criteria and special education eligibility criteria, legal issues such as capital punishment, theories of intelligence, test instruments used in the assessment of an intellectual disability, and postassessment planning. In addition, they illustrate in sample reports how assessment data can be integrated in a brief report in order to inform treatment and guide interventions.

Alan S. Kaufman, PhD, and Nadeen L. Kaufman, EdD, Series Editors
Yale Child Study Center, Yale University School of Medicine

ACKNOWLEDGMENTS

We would like to thank Marquita Flemming, Senior Editor at Wiley, for all of her assistance. She provided a great deal of help and support – from project inception to the final manuscript – and always offered great feedback. We are grateful to have worked with her.

Essentials of Intellectual Disability Assessment and Identification

One

HISTORY OF INTELLECTUAL DISABILITY

This introductory chapter provides a brief but significant discussion concerning how intellectual disability (ID) has been defined and conceptualized historically by the different classification systems: *Diagnostic and Statistical Manual of Mental Disorders (DSM)*, American Association on Mental Retardation/American Association on Intellectual and Developmental Disabilities (AAMR/AAIDD), and Individuals with Disabilities Education Act (IDEA). This background information lays the foundation for a more complete understanding of issues associated with the diagnosis of intellectual disability and the evolution that has occurred in the ways the disorder is conceptualized today. This chapter will discuss the shift in conceptualization from variations in the degree to which the disorder is manifested (*DSM*: mild, moderate, severe, profound) to variations in the intensity of services needed (AAIDD: intermittent, limited, extensive, pervasive). The 2010 *AAIDD Operational Definition of Intellectual Disability* is addressed.

EARLY BEGINNINGS

Historically, distinctions between "idiots" and the "insane" began to emerge out of necessity, at the end of the Middle Ages, as laws were being developed. Within this context, idiots were thought to be less responsible for crimes committed resulting from their lack understanding due to their state of ignorance. On the other hand, those who were insane had the ability to understand and plan but committed crimes based on their lack of adherence to moral standards, which was considered an offence that was punishable by law (Wickman, 2013). However, the first reported documentation of the distinction between mental capacity and mental illness came in 1838, when the scientist Jean Esquirol

(1772–1810) published his manuscript on mental health. In his book, Esquirol devoted a large section to the topic of idiocy and stated that there was a distinction between an "idiot", who is never able to develop his or her mental capacity, and a "mentally deranged" person, who developed normal intellectual ability but then had lost it (Sattler, 2001, p. 129). Later it was recognized that Esquirol's description of the characteristics of those with idiocy closely matched features of what we currently know as Down syndrome (Roubertouz & Kerdelhue, 2006).

The system of care and support for individuals with intellectual disabilities had its roots in the beginning of the 19th century with Jean Itard's attempts to educate Victor (the wild boy of Aveyron), a boy in his early teens who had been living on his own in the forest. Although Itard eventually abandoned his efforts due to slow progress and minimal gains, he did open the door for future efforts in the intervention and training of skills in individuals with intellectual disabilities. By the mid-1800s, advocates such as Cheyne Brady, a London lawyer, published a volume titled *What Can Be Done for the Idiot*, in which he wrote that although idiocy is "unquestionably one of the most fearful of the host of maladies," modern science shows the promise that "there is no class of unfortunates of our species to whom enlightened treatment may be applied with a more cheering hope of success" (Brady, as cited in Ferguson, Ferguson, & Wehmeyer, 2013, p. 87).

In 1840, medical student and educationalist Edouard Seguin, who worked with Victor under Itard's direction, established the first private school in Paris dedicated to the education of individuals with intellectual disabilities. In 1846, he published *Traitement Moral, Hygiène, et Education des Idiots* (The Moral Treatment, Hygiene, and Education of Idiots and Other Backward Children). Seguin created a program, called the *Physiological Method,* which was a sensory-based training program (dealing with vision, hearing, taste, smell, touch) developed to enhance the senses and potentially open the channels to increased cognitive functioning (Sheerenberger, 1983). He later expanded the program to include memory, imitation, reinforcement, and vocational training. Sequin relocated to the United States in 1850, where he continued to revolutionize education for individuals with intellectual disabilities. In 1876, he became the founding father of the American Association on Mental Retardation (AAMR). The next section outlines the history of intellectual disabilities, previously known as mental retardation (MR). Some of the key milestones in the historical progression are highlighted in **Rapid Reference 1.1.**

≡ *Rapid Reference 1.1 A Historical Look at Intellectual Disabilities*

....

1838 Jean Esquirol publishes a manuscript which contains a large section devoted to determining the difference between idiocy and mentally deranged persons.

1876 Seguin becomes the founding father of AAMR.

1905 The Binet Simon, published in France, becomes the first instrument to assess intelligence.

1910 AAMR publishes the first system of classification for MR. Henry Goddard, director of research at the Vineland Training School, publishes an American version of the Binet Simon.

1916 Terman renames the Binet-Simon the Stanford Binet and revises how intelligence is derived using the intelligence quotient (IQ).

1935 Edgar Doll publishes the Vineland Social Maturity Scale.

1952 *DSM–I* (American Psychiatric Association [APA]) introduces the classification category of *mental deficiency* for cases primarily presenting as a defect in intelligence. The category contains three levels of severity: mild, moderate, and severe.

1959 AAMR announces three criteria for establishing MR: low IQ (less than 85), impaired adaptive behavior, and onset before age 16. Five levels of severity are suggested: borderline, mild, moderate, severe, and profound.

1968 *DSM–II* (APA) changes the name from "mental deficiency" to "mental retardation" and adopts the five levels of severity suggested by the AAMR. Criteria are low IQ (less than 85), impaired adaptive skills, and onset during the developmental period.

1971 In *Wyatt v. Stickney*, a landmark class action suit in Alabama, Judge Johnson rules that individuals confined to residential centers have a right to treatment.

1975 Public Law 94-142: Rights of all children with disabilities to have a free and appropriate education. The law, The Education of all Handicapped Children Act (EHA), provides state grants for the provision of services for children with disabilities.

1979 As a result of the class action lawsuit *Larry P. v. Riles*, all California school districts were barred from using IQ tests as the sole means of determining placement of African American children in classes for the educable mentally retarded.

1980 *DSM–III* (APA) reduced "subnormal" intelligence from an IQ of 85 (1 standard deviation [SD] below the mean) to an IQ of 70 (2 SDs below the mean).

1990 EHA is revised and renamed the Individuals with Disabilities Education Act (IDEA).

1992 AAMR releases the revision of its manual replacing levels of severity of MR with patterns and intensity of supports needed: intermittent, limited, extensive, and pervasive.

1994 *DSM–IV* (APA) retains the four levels of severity—mild, moderate, severe, profound—which are no longer comparable to AAMR criteria; however, it makes comparisons to the education system (e.g., "mild" is equivalent to "educable"; "moderate" is equivalent to "trainable").

1997 IDEA is reauthorized.

2004 IDEA reauthorized and renamed the Individuals with Disabilities Education Improvement Act of 2004.

2007 AAMR changes its name to the American Association on Individuals with Intellectual and Developmental Disabilities (AAIDD).

2010 President Obama signs "Rosa's Law" on October 5.

2010 AAIDD publishes the most recent version, the 11th edition of AAIDD's *Intellectual Disability: Definition, Classification, and Systems of Support* (AAIDD, 2010).

2013 *DSM–5* (APA) publishes the most recent criteria for intellectual disability in the section on Neurodevelopmental Disorders.

THE TURN OF THE CENTURY: 1900 TO 1950

In the United States, Samuel Gridley Howe, who had worked with children who were blind and deaf-blind, began to look for ways to bring this sense of optimism from Europe to the Western world and emphasized the importance of identifying levels of idiocy. He suggested that the levels ranged from pure idiocy (the most severe form) to fools and simpletons, whom he felt had the best chances for improvement, based on education and training (Ferguson et al., 2013). In the wake of the Industrial Revolution and the influx of many street children into the schools, the French government commissioned Alfred Binet (1857–1911), a lawyer and scientist, and Theodore Simon (1873–1961) to develop a method of screening which children might be identified as "mentally retarded" in order to better assist these children with special education interventions at school. The measurement, the Binet-Simon Scales (1905), became the first instrument of its kind to identify the degree of MR based on an individual's response to a series of age-based questions (Sattler, 2001). However, by the beginning of the 20th century, optimism was replaced by a growing pessimism that, unlike insanity, idiocy or feeblemindedness was not a disease but a defect that could not be cured. With this attitude came the transformation of institutions of training into warehouses of custodial care (Ferguson et al., 2013).

Henry Goddard (1866–1957), who was the director of training at the Vineland Training School in New Jersey, published an English version of the Binet-Simon scale in 1910. However, his use of the instrument was based on his firm belief that intelligence was an inherited disposition which was not curable, and his sole purpose for giving the test was to identify those who were "feeble-minded" (Nietzel, Bernstein, & Milich, 1994). The rise of institutions also foreshadowed the demise of the family unit for many children, who were taken from families and placed in institutions/asylums under the guise of the "child's best interest," thus placing blame for their "defect" on the family environment, which was often impoverished. In a transition to a less humane and pessimistic outlook, "the goal was to remediate if possible, but to incarcerate in any case. Custody had replaced cure; therapy had become control" (Ferguson et al., 2013, p. 112).

DON'T FORGET

Goddard spent considerable time researching the history of families with "feebleminded" offspring. One of the most famous studies was his research on the Kallikak family that traced two sets of children born to Martin Kallikak from his liaison with a feebleminded tavern girl and later a Quaker woman from a good family. While all offspring from the tavern girl were plagued with feeblemindedness and other sordid outcomes (epilepsy, lechery, alcoholism), all offspring from the Quaker woman were successful members of society. While some professors were impressed by Goddard's studies, there was a mixed reaction from the scientific community (Zenderland, 2004). However, the studies' influence on the eugenicist movement, which brought compulsory sterilization laws in 30 states, cannot be underrated.

At this time in the United States, terms like "feeblemindedness" and "mental deficiency" were commonly used to refer to those who had MR. However, in 1910, the American Association on Mental Retardation (AAMR) developed what would become the first system of classification for MR. AAMR announced that arrested development, which resulted in feeblemindedness, should be identified based on the individual's level of functioning: the term "idiot" was reserved for those who had a developmental level equivalent to 2 years of age; "imbecile" was reserved for those who functioned between 2 and 7 years of age; and "moron" was used for those with a mental age equivalent between 7 and 12 years of age (Biasini, Grupe, Juffman, & Bray, 1999).

With an increased need to better identify levels of MR, Terman revised the Binet scales, renaming them the Stanford-Binet (1916), and incorporated the idea of relating mental age to chronological age, or what he termed the "intelligence quotient (IQ)," which represented the ratio of the child's mental age to his or her chronological age. Through the use of the IQ score, it would now be possible to compare two children of the same age who were functioning at very different levels. After many revisions, the ratio IQ was replaced by a more sophisticated method of calculation based on the deviation IQ.

DON'T FORGET

Terman's original formula for obtaining the IQ score was to divide mental age by chronological age and multiply by 100. Using the original formula, we can compare Sally, Suzy, and Sarah, each of whom is 8 years old. On an IQ test, Sally has a mental age of 10, Suzy has a mental age of 8, and Sarah has a mental age of 6. Based on Terman's formula, Sally would have an IQ of (10 / 8 x 100) 125; Suzy would have an IQ of (8 / 8 x 100) 100; and Sarah would have an IQ of (6 / 8 x 100) 75. In this case, Sally, who is 8 years old and functioning at her age level, has an IQ of 100, which is the average IQ score.

THE AGE OF ASSESSMENT: LATE 1950S TO 1970

In 1950, over 124,000 individuals lived in state institutions for the mentally retarded. By 1967, the number had escalated to over 194,000 individuals (Wehmeyer & Schalock, 2013). Overcrowding and poor resources eventually led to discontent with large institutions, and communities began to provide more local services. The growing trend toward deinstitutionalization came at a time when there was increasing visibility of disabilities in the numbers of disabled war veterans returning to the United States at the end of World War II.

In 1950, representatives from 23 parent groups formed the National Association of Parents and Friends of Mentally Retarded Children in Minneapolis, Minnesota (currently called The Arc of the United States), and by 1975 the organization had 214,000 members (Wehmeyer & Schalock, 2013). Although initially focused on reducing the stigma associated with intellectual disabilities and raising awareness that children with mental disabilities were innocent and deserving of love, as the children grew into adulthood, advocates fought for the rights of these individuals as citizens, and the name of the association changed in 1975 to the National Associated for Retarded Citizens to reflect this trend.

By the end of the 1950s, the AAMR announced full support for expanding the criteria for the identification of individuals with MR beyond the sole criterion of the IQ score to include:

- an IQ score of less than 85;
- impairment in adaptive behavior; and
- onset prior to 18 years of age.

Although the Vineland Social Maturity Scale had been available for some time, at this time estimates of adaptive behavior were made based on subjective reports.

DON'T FORGET

When the AAMR announced the three criteria, it also advanced the identification process by naming five different levels of MR:

1. Borderline (IQ 67–83)
2. Mild Retardation (IQ 50–66)
3. Moderate Retardation (IQ 33–49)
4. Severe Retardation (IQ 16–32)
5. Profound Retardation (IQ < 16) (Heber, 1961)

These five levels of severity were introduced into the DSM–II (APA, 1968).

By the mid-1960s, increasing numbers of children were being tested and placed in residential centers as attitudes shifted from prevention and treatment to identification and placement. At that time, a university professor, Burton Blatt, and his friend and photographer Fred Kaplan published a photographic essay titled *Christmas in Purgatory: A Photographic Essay of Mental Retardation* (Blatt & Kaplan, 1966). The volume described state institutions as "human warehouses" filled with children and adults who were mentally retarded. Mental health issues were placed on the back burners since the prevailing mind-set was that children were miniature adults and that they were either too young to experience mental disorders, or, if they did, then these disorders would be experienced in the same way as adults.

During the 20-year span from 1950 to 1970, advocacy groups lobbied for the rights of individuals with MR, culminating in such Federal court class-action lawsuits as the *Wyatt-Stickney* federal court case in Alabama in the 1970s, which established the right to treatment for individuals living in residential facilities and made purely custodial care unacceptable (Biasini et al., 1999). In addition, the growing opposition and concern of the overrepresentation of minority children in special education led to changes in the criteria for MR, lowering the IQ to 70 from 85 (Grossman, 1973). It was during this time period that the famous case of *Larry P. v. Riles* surfaced in the California courts, resulting in an injunction preventing the San Francisco school district from using IQ scores to place black children in special education classes for the educable mentally retarded. The result was that the school district was no longer allowed to justify placement in special education classes based on IQ score alone.

DON'T FORGET

The IQ test is based on the standard distribution with an average IQ of 100 and an SD of 15. Approximately 68% of the population will score within 1 SD of the mean (e.g., IQ 85–115). The drop in IQ score from 85 to 70 meant a shift that would require an individual to score 2 SDs below the mean on an IQ test to be within the MR Range. Approximately 2% of the population would obtain an IQ of 70 or less.

Increased pressure to acknowledge the rights of children with disabilities to have a free and appropriate education resulted in the passing of Public Law (P.L.) 94-142 in 1975, which supported the AAMR initiatives to include adaptive measures as part of the process of identifying children with MR in the educational system. The law, titled the Education of All Handicapped Children Act (EHA), was instrumental in legislating grants to fund educational programs for children with disabilities. The law has seen several revisions and was renamed the Individuals with Disabilities Education Act (IDEA) in 1990 and was most recently reauthorized and renamed the Individuals with Disabilities Education Improvement Act of 2004 (IDEA, 2005) (Wilmshurst & Brue, 2010).

1980S TO THE PRESENT

Although the current status of intellectual disability will be discussed in depth in Chapter 3, this section will provide a brief update as to the shift in thinking that has led to changes in the way that intellectual disability is currently conceptualized. This shift is best understood by addressing the definitions and criteria within the context of three different classification systems: *DSM*, AAMR/AAIDD, and IDEA.

Diagnostic and Statistical Manual of Mental Disorders (DSM)

When the *DSM* was first released in 1952, the classification category of *mental deficiency* was introduced to account for "those cases presenting primarily a defect of intelligence existing since birth, without demonstrated organic brain disease or known prenatal cause." Cases were to include only individuals with familial or idiopathic (unknown origin) mental deficiencies, and severity was to be determined by IQ scores in the following three ranges: *mild* (an IQ of approximately 70–85); *moderate* (IQ 50–70); *severe* (IQs below 50). Although IQ scores were necessary to determine the range and expectations, the *DSM* noted the importance of considering other factors and emphasized that "The degree of defect is estimated from other factors than merely psychological test scores, namely, consideration of cultural, physical and emotional determinants, as well as school, vocational and social effectiveness" (APA, 1952, pp. 23–24). Alternatively, an individual could be diagnosed with chronic brain syndrome with mental deficiency, in cases where "This categorization relegates the defect of intelligence to the sphere of symptomatology, rather than recognizing it as a primary mental disturbance" (APA, 1952, p. 10). However, in this first attempt to define the disorder, the *DSM* made it clear that the terms used were not completely satisfactory:

> An unsuccessful attempt was made to find a substitute for the long used term "mental deficiency." Mental deficiency is a legal term, comparable to the term "insanity," it has little meaning in clinical psychiatry. The term has been defined by law in England, and in some parts of the United States. The same objection is raised to the terms "idiot," "imbecile," and "moron." They have the further fault of being based upon psychological testing alone. In the borderline areas of each term, groupings vary with the immediate condition of the patient, as well as with the skill and training of the examiner. These last named terms have been eliminated.
>
> *(APA, 1952, p. 10).*

In the next revision of the *DSM* (APA, 1968), the term "mental retardation" replaced "mentally deficient." At this time, the *DSM–II* better aligned with the AAMR and also supported five ranges of severity—borderline, mild, moderate, severe, and profound—with the borderline range for IQ scores in the 68 to 85 range. There was an additional category, called "Unspecified MR," which was defined as "subnormal general intellectual functioning which originates during the developmental period and is associated with impairment of either learning and social adjustment or maturation, or both" (APA, 1968, p. 14).

The *DSM* spent considerable effort listing clinical codes for 9 subcategories for the disorder, based on the circumstances of origin (e.g., following infection and intoxication; following trauma or physical agent, etc.). The *DSM–III* (APA, 1980) introduced a new chapter to the manual specific to "Disorders Usually First Evident in Infancy, Childhood, or Adolescence" and MR was placed in this section. The three main criteria for a diagnosis of MR remained consistent with the previous version (e.g., impaired IQ, impaired adaptive behaviors, and onset during the developmental period); however, these criteria were further refined at this time. Subnormal intelligence was now set 2 *SDs* below the mean (IQ of 70) instead of 1 *SD* (IQ of 85), with the addition of a five-point interval to be considered (IQ 65–75) to account for the standard error of measure. Onset during the developmental period was defined as occurring before 18 years of age. Impairments in adaptive functioning were required; however, the *DSM* noted that current measures were not considered valid to be used in isolation to make this decision and recommended that clinical judgment should evaluate adaptive functioning in individuals relative to similar-aged peers.

In the fourth revision of the classification manual, the *DSM–IV* (APA, 1994), MR was retained in the section on "Disorders Usually First Diagnosed in Childhood or Adolescence." The decision was made to code MR on Axis II of the Five Axis System, along with the personality disorders, to avoid not giving the disorder enough recognition, if the focus was on another primary disorder occurring on Axis I.

DON'T FORGET

The text revision of the *DSM–IV* (*DSM–IV–TR*; APA, 2000) specified four different ranges of severity for MR based on the IQ score:

Mild MR: IQ 50–55 to approximately 70
Moderate MR: IQ 35–40 to 50–55
Severe MR: IQ 20–25 to 35–40
Profound MR: IQ below 20–25

The four ranges of severity represented a change from the five ranges of the *DSM–II* (APA, 1968) and retained the change to four ranges proposed in the *DSM–III* (APA, 1980).

The three core criteria were retained from the previous revision; however, the criteria of adaptive functioning was further defined as requiring deficits in

2 of 10 possible areas—functional academic skills, social/interpersonal skills, communication skills, self-care, home living, use of community resources, self-direction, work, leisure and health/safety—as determined by an individual's score on an adaptive measure that was two standard deviations below the norm. These criteria remained consistent in the subsequent text revision of the *DSM*, *DSM–IV–TR* (APA, 2000).

There have been many changes in the way that disorders have been conceptualized in the most recent revision of the *DSM*: *DSM–5* (APA, 2013). In an attempt to move away from a purely categorical classification system and to incorporate more of a dimensional approach to regarding disorders along a continuum, the *DSM* has organized the manual based on a developmental framework. The section on "Disorders Usually First Diagnosed in Childhood or Adolescence" has been removed and in its place a new section, on "Neurodevelopmental Disorders," has been added.

The term "mental retardation" (MR) has been replaced by "intellectual disabilities (ID)," also known as "intellectual developmental disorders (IDD)," which include categories for global developmental delay (for children under 5 years of age who demonstrate delays and have not yet been assessed) and unspecified intellectual disability (for cases over 5 years of age where assessment cannot be conducted due to other factors, such as severe behavior problems or sensory/motor impairments). The *DSM–5* (APA 2013) continues to use specifiers to identify the severity of the disorder; however, unlike previous versions of the *DSM*, the severity no longer is based on IQ scores but now refers to levels of adaptive functioning in the conceptual, social, and pragmatic domains. The current *DSM* criteria are discussed in depth in Chapter 3.

AAMR/AAIDD

Throughout the course of history, the AAMR has been a vital force in shaping how MR has been conceptualized. In 1992, the organization made a controversial decision to shift the emphasis from focusing on the severity of the disorder—mild, moderate, severe, and profound—to focusing on the intensity of services that are required to provide the necessary supports: intermittent, limited, extensive, or pervasive. As a result, the definition for MR took on a more applied focus, and the defining feature of "substantial limitations in present functioning" was described as including "significant subaverage functioning, existing concurrently with limitations in two or more of the following applicable adaptive skill areas: communication, self-care, home living, social skills, community use, self direction, health and safety functional academics, leisure and work" (Luckasson et al.,

2002). This definition also stated that onset of MR had to be prior to 18 years of age; this was an increase of 2 years from the previous definition, which had onset prior to 16 years of age.

The definition for MR continued to evolve. In 2002, the AAMR released the 10th revision of *MR: Definition, Classification and Systems of Support* (Luckasson et al., 2002). This revision built on changes made in the 10 years earlier but also made a strong statement that caused further separation from how MR was conceptualized in the *DSM–IV–TR*. The AAMR emphasized that even though MR was contained in the *DSM*, it should not be considered a mental disorder; instead, it should be conceptualized as "a state of functioning" beginning in childhood that is characterized by limitations in intellectual and adaptive skills. Within this framework, the focus was shifting toward greater recognition of the individual strengths and weaknesses and the ecological influences that can help shape interventions in the conceptual, social, and practical adaptive areas of development.

In keeping with its focus on advocating for the rights of those with MR, in 2007 the AAMR made a landmark decision to change the name of the disorder from "mental retardation" to "intellectual and developmental disability" (IDD). It then followed suit by changing the name of the organization to the American Association on Intellectual and Developmental Disabilities (AAIDD; Schalock et al., 2007). In October 2010, President Barack Obama signed "Rosa's Law" (P.L. 111-156), which authorized the use of the term "intellectual disability" to replace the term "mental retardation" in all federal, health, and labor laws.

DON'T FORGET

The most recent definition for intellectual disability is a concise definition that emphasizes the three diagnostic criteria:

1. Significant limitations of intellectual functioning
2. Significant limitations in adaptive behavior
3. Onset during the developmental period

The most recent revision of the definition can be found in the 11th edition of AAIDD's *Intellectual Disability: Definition, Classification and Systems of Supports* (AAIDD, 2010). Main ideas found in this revision are summarized in the "Don't Forget" box and will be discussed, at length, in Chapter 3.

AAIDD continues to emphasize a supports-based definition for intellectual disability, which is a condition characterized by significant limitations in intellectual functioning and adaptive behavior. The problems must have originated during one's developmental period.

This definition is based on five assumptions, the last two of which emphasize supports:

1. Limitations in present functioning must be considered within the context of the individual's community with regard to age/peers/culture.
2. Assessment must recognize the importance of cultural and linguistic diversity as well as limitations in communication, sensory, motor, and behavior.
3. Within an individual, limitations often coexist with strengths.
4. The purpose of describing limitations is to develop a profile to assist with the planning of needed supports.
5. Appropriate personalized supports over time will generally lead to improved quality of life for the individual. (AAIDD, 2010, p. 7)

Although historically, classification was based on IQ scores, Schalock et al. (2012) emphasized that the nature of contemporary questions, such as queries concerning issues of competency, place IQ on the "wayside," and draw increased attention to multidimensional aspects of classification, including intellect, adaptation, health, participation, and context. The concept of intellectual disability proposed in the AAIDD's 2010 manual is discussed in greater depth in Chapter 3.

Education System and Special Education Law

In 1975, the Education for All Handicapped Children Act (EHA) came into effect with the passing of P.L. 94-142, which provided federally funded programs and services for children with disabilities from 3 to 21 years of age. Although the *DSM* and AAMR were working toward aligning their definitions for MR, the educational system based its classification on children's predicted ability to learn (Kirk, Karnes, & Kirk, 1955). Children were considered *educable* if they could learn simple academic skills that did not progress above a fourth-grade level. Children were considered *trainable* if they could learn simple self-care skills but could learn very few academic skills. Children were considered *untrainable* if they were totally dependent on others or required custodial care, such as a residential setting.

In 1990, EHA was renamed the Individuals with Disabilities Education Act (IDEA). In 2004, when the act was reauthorized, it was renamed the Individuals with Disabilities Education Improvement Act, and was passed into law in 2005. The US Department of Education (DOE) is responsible for insuring that public schools comply with educational rights and laws (IDEA, 2004) and laws related to civil liberties (Americans with Disabilities Act Amendments Act of 2008 and

Section 504 of the Rehabilitation Act of 1973). IDEA 2004 is responsible for special education (individualized education programs [IEPs]) and related services (e.g., speech and language therapy, physical and occupational therapy, counseling) for children who meet criteria for one of the 13 categories of exceptionalities. Mental retardation is one of the 13 categories of exceptionalities listed under IDEA. However, with the passing of Rosa's Law in 2010, the term "intellectual disability," initially adopted by AAIDD (AAIDD, 2010), is growing throughout federal law. Rosa's Law "replaced the terms mental retardation and mentally retarded with intellectual disability and intellectually disabled in federal health, education, and labor statutes. These statutes include such critical laws as the Public Health Service Act, the Individuals with Disabilities Education Act (IDEA), and the Rehabilitation Act (Ford, Acosta, & Sutcliffe, 2013, p. 109). Since the vast majority of individuals with intellectual disabilities fall within the mild range (scores ranging from 50 to 70), it is most likely that these individuals will be serviced by schools in the local community and meet criteria for special education and related services under IDEA. As a result, the most recent reauthorization of the law has incorporated efforts to enhance the identification and intervention procedures. The law has four main parts: Parts A and B focus on the eligibility criteria of children 3 to 21 years of age; Part C targets services for infants and toddlers with disabilities under 3 years of age; and Part D addresses national activities that have been developed to enhance education services for children with disabilities. How these sections apply specifically to children with an intellectual disability and developmental delays is discussed in greater detail in Chapter 3.

SUMMARY

It becomes increasingly evident that our understanding of intellectual disabilities has evolved historically through the work of advocates and families who have fought for the rights of individuals with intellectual abilities and who have fought against the stigma that was initially attached to this disorder. With the advent of the intelligence test in the early 1900s, educators and psychologists were able to identify which children had intellectual disabilities and, hopefully, remediate and enhance skills by placement in residential training programs. However, there was disillusionment with the lack of success of these programs that often provided only custodial care. Through movements such as the National Association of Retarded Citizens (ARC) and the President's Commission on Mental Retardation in the 1970s, laws were passed to protect and preserve the rights of those with an intellectual disability to receive appropriate treatment in residential facilities. However, disfavor with the residential system resulted in many of the children with an intellectual disability seeking placement in local community schools. With the passing of P.L. 94-142-142, the right to a free and appropriate public education was now properly funded and guaranteed for children with disabilities. During this time, and for several years to follow, identification and definitions for individuals with an intellectual disability would continue to reflect changes in criteria and terminology used by the medical profession (APA), advocacy organizations (AAMR/AADID), and the educational system.

🪶 TEST YOURSELF 🪶

1. In the mid-1800s, this individual was one of the first to develop a program, the *Physiological Method*, to enhance sensory skills in those with intellectual disabilities. He later relocated to the United States and became the founding father of AAMR.
   (a) Jean Itard
   (b) Eduard Seguin
   (c) Cheyne Brady
   (d) Jean Esquirol

2. In 1910, the AAMR published the first system of classification for intellectual disabilities. Which of the following is true regarding that system?
   (a) The term "idiot" was reserved for those with a developmental level equivalent to 2 years of age.
   (b) The term "moron" was reserved for those with a mental age equivalent between 2 and 7 years of age.
   (c) The term "imbecile" was reserved for those with a mental age equivalent between 7 and 12 years of age.
   (d) The term "feeblemindedness" was replaced by "mental deficiency."

3. All of the following are true about Goddard's legacy, except:
   (a) he researched the Kallikak family, finding two strains of offspring: the feebleminded and others who were successful members of society.
   (b) he published an English version of the Binet-Simon Scale.
   (c) he was an advocate for the rights of the feebleminded to have fair and equal opportunities, and he developed programs to reverse feeblemindedness.
   (d) he was the director of training at the Vineland Training School.

4. In the late 1950s, AAMR expanded the criteria for the identification of individuals with mental retardation. Which of the following was included in the expanded criteria?
   (a) An IQ of less than 85
   (b) Impairment in adaptive behavior
   (c) Onset prior to 18 years of age
   (d) All of the above

5. **In 1970s, the *Wyatt- Stickney* federal court case in Alabama established the right to:**
    (a) a free and appropriate education.
    (b) treatment for individuals in residential facilities.
    (c) vote for individuals with disabilities.
    (d) legal counsel for individuals with disabilities.

6. **In the *DSM–IV* (APA, 1994), the important decision was made to:**
    (a) increase the number of categories (ranges of severity) from four to five.
    (b) decrease the IQ cutoff from an IQ of 70 to an IQ of 85.
    (c) code MR on Axis II of the Five Axis System, along with the personality disorders.
    (d) merge the severity categories of Mild and Moderate Severity to the category of Minimal Severity to increase the prevalence of individuals in the upper level of the disability.

7. **In 2002, the AAMR released the 10th revision of its manual, which emphasized a significant difference in the way MR was conceptualized by this advocacy group and the *DSM*. The AAMR emphasized:**
    (a) that MR was not a "mental disorder" but "a state of functioning."
    (b) a shift in emphasis from weaknesses to patterns of individual strengths and weaknesses.
    (c) increased focus on ecological influences and interventions.
    (d) all of the above.

8. **With the passing of "Rosa's Law," what major change was made?**
    (a) The developmental age for identification of intellectual disability was increased from 18 to 21.
    (b) Individuals with intellectual disabilities were given the right to treatment.
    (c) The terms "mental retardation" and "mentally retarded" were replaced with "intellectual disability" or "intellectual developmental disability."
    (d) Gender discrimination for those with intellectual disabilities was given increased awareness.

Answers: 1. b; 2. a; 3. c; 4. d; 5. b; 6. c; 7. d; 8. c.

Two

PREVALENCE, CAUSES, ISSUES, AND COMORBID DISORDERS

n this chapter, we provide a brief overview of intellectual disability (ID) or intellectual developmental disorder (IDD), the different types of etiology for the disorders (chromosomal abnormalities/genetic origins and environmental toxins/teratogens), and the common types of intellectual disabilities associated with each factor: chromosomal (Down syndrome, Williams syndrome, Prader-Willi syndrome, Angelman syndrome) and environmental (fetal alcohol syndrome, teratogens, alcohol, lead-based paint, etc.). We also supply information on prevalence rates and descriptions of the common characteristics associated with each disorder type. The remainder of the chapter will focus on such topics as distinguishing between an intellectual disability and a developmental delay and other differential diagnoses, such as *autism spectrum disorders* (ASD), *learning disabilities* (such as dyslexia, dyscalculia, dyspraxia/developmental coordination disorder, dysgraphia), or other early onset disorders, such as *language impairments* (including late language emergence (LLE), *specific language impairment* (SLI, or selective mutism). Some of the more common comorbid disorders will be addressed in Chapter 3.

ETIOLOGY OF INTELLECTUAL DISABILITIES: SUBTYPES

Intellectual disabilities can have a wide range of etiology including innate factors (genetic factors and biological) that are often outside of one's control, and environmental factors that are often preventable (toxins in the environment, or *teratogens*). As a result of the Human Genome Project and advances in human genetics, our knowledge and understanding of the influences that gene variants can have on human development and the potential for increased risks for vulnerability for some conditions have increased significantly. As noted by Khoury, Burke, and Thomson (2000), "Risks for almost all human diseases result from the interactions between inherited gene variants and environmental factors, including chemical, physical, and infectious agents and behavioral or nutritional factors.

17

which raises the possibility of targeting disease prevention and health promotion efforts to individuals at risk because of their genetic make-up (p 5)." At the time of publication of their book on genetics and public health, 872 genes had been identified that could increase the risk of having an intellectual disability (Khoury et al., 2000).

In this section, we will discuss two broad areas of etiology: an intellectual disability due to genetic conditions and chromosome abnormalities, and an intellectual disability resulting from environmental factors.

Intellectual Disabilities Due to Genetic and Chromosomal Abnormalities

Individuals whose intellectual disability results from biological causes have either inherited a genetic defect or develop a chromosomal abnormality (genes combine or mutate or are compromised in some way). The following are some of the most common types of intellectual disability that result from genetic and chromosomal causes.

Down Syndrome. With a worldwide annual prevalence rate of 1 in every 1,000 births and a US prevalence rate of 1 in 800 births, Down syndrome (DS) is one of the most common chromosome abnormalities found in humans (Weijerman & de Winter, 2010). DS results from anomalies with chromosome 21. There are several ways that this gene can be compromised: An extra chromosome 21 may be evident, or the chromosome itself may be damaged in some way. Those with DS who have an extra chromosome are called Trisomy 21. The extra chromosome can cause a host of physical problems and cognitive challenges (Grant, 2006).

Individuals with DS are not a homogeneous group, and characteristics can differ widely, since not all features of DS are present in every case. However, some of the more typical traits include: short stature; short, broad hands and feet; round face; almond-shaped eyes; low muscle tone; flat facial features; and a protruding tongue (Perkins, 2009). In addition to unique physical characteristics, children with DS may also experience problems with motor skills (poor coordination and fine motor development) and speech (grammar, expressive language and articulation). Grammatical skills can be very weak (Fowler, 1990), and expressive language disabilities have been reported to be evident in as high as 83% to 100% of children with DS (Miller, 1999). Many parents of children with DS report that articulation problems often result in outsiders not being able to understand what the child is saying (Kumin, 1994). Despite these limitations, children with DS can be socially engaging and affectionate and have strong imitative skills, although they can also exhibit occasional stubborn tendencies. Individuals with DS may be vulnerable to a number of medical issues. Almost 50% of those born with DS also have congenital heart disease (Freeman et al., 1998) while between 38% and 78% will suffer from hearing loss (Roizen, Walters, Nicol, & Blondis, 1993).

The majority of children with DS will exhibit limitations in intellectual ability. They may be functioning within the intellectual range of 30 to 70, with an average IQ of 50 (Vicari, 2005). Some children with DS, however, are able to score within the upper limits of the low average range (IQ 85–90), which is referred to as "upper level DS." Children who are diagnosed with upper level DS may not meet criteria for a *DSM* diagnosis of an intellectual disability. Although there is wide variability in IQ levels for individuals with DS, research has demonstrated that overall IQ level progressively declines with age (Pennington, Moon, Edgin, Stedron, & Nadel, 2003).

There is an increased risk of bearing a child with DS as the mother or father ages. Research has demonstrated that prior to a woman being 35 years of age there is minimal evidence of increased risk for having a child with DS. However, the odds progress rapidly after 35 years of age. For example, a woman at age 20 has 1 in 1,441 chance of having a child with DS. This increases to 1 in 959 by 30 years of age. But by 40 years of age, the chances increase to 1 in 84, and by 50, the increase rises to 1 in 44 births (Morris, Mutton, & Alberman, 2002). Once maternal age reaches 40, then paternal age seems to take on more influence and now accounts for 50% of the influence on birth risk (Fisch et al., 2003).

DON'T FORGET

Although the prevalence rate for Down syndrome is 1 in 800 births, when maternal age hits 40, the influences of maternal and paternal age can increase that risk by almost 10 percent (e.g., 1 in 800 to 1 in 84 births).

Prader-Willi Syndrome. The prevalence rate for Prader-Willi syndrome (PWS) is in the range of 1 in 15,000 to 1 in 30,000 births (Cassidy & Driscoll, 2008). Children born with Prader-Willi syndrome will have a defect on chromosome 15. This defect is passed down from the father and results in a number of associated characteristics, including intellectual impairment. Developmental delay is often detected soon after birth due to low muscle tone and low reflexes (Milner et al., 2005).

Cassidy and Driscoll (2008) reported that milestones are very delayed, with attainment taking about twice the time compared to a normally developing child; examples are sitting at age 12 months (instead of 6 months), walking at age 24 months (instead of 1 year), and speaking words at age 2 years (instead of 1 year). Cognitive disabilities in children with PWS will be identified early in the school program. The majority of children with PWS fall within the range of mild intellectual disability (mean IQ: 60 to 70), while 40% will score within the borderline range (IQ: 70 to 80) or within the range of low-average intelligence (IQ: 80 to 90). About 20% will have an IQ score that falls within the moderate range of intellectual disability (IQ: 40 to 60) (Malich, Largo, Schinzel, Molinari, & Eiholzer, 2000).

Physically, children with Prader-Willi syndrome are often short in stature and have small hands and feet (Dykens & Cassidy, 1995). The syndrome is often accompanied by a triad of symptoms, including: maladaptive behavior (impulsivity, temper tantrums, mood swings, aggression, and compulsive eating), obsessive-compulsive characteristics, and skin picking (Dykens & Cassidy, 1995; Wigren & Hanson, 2005). Compulsive eating can result in weight gain, and behavioral controls are often required to combat obesity.

Angelman Syndrome. The prevalence rate for Angelman syndrome (AS) is estimated to be between 1 in 10,000 to 1 in 40,000 births (Clayton-Smith & Laan, 2003). Children born with AS also have a defect on chromosome 15, but this time it is passed on by the mother. Epileptic seizures can be common in children with AS, occurring in about 80% of the population. Seizures, if present, often will have onset between 1 and 5 years of age and resemble epilepsy with febrile convulsions in infancy (Clayton-Smith & Laan, 2003).

Children with AS also may have odd physical features, such as a flattened and microcephalic head. The syndrome was once called the "happy puppet syndrome" to capture the inappropriate smiling/laughter that accompanies the syndrome (Horsler & Oliver, 2006). Researchers have consistently identified four symptom clusters that characterize the syndrome: inappropriate affect (frequent and inappropriate laughing/smiling), developmental delay, speech delay, and movement disorders (Horsler & Oliver, 2006).

Children with AS have severe intellectual disability. Milestones are delayed, some significantly, with sitting occurring around 12 months, crawling at 18 to 24 months, and walking at a mean age of 4 years (Clayton-Smith, 1993). It has become clearer that the clinical spectrum of AS can be more variable than initially conceptualized. Many individuals do not have all the physical characteristics, seizures are not present in every case, and some speech may be present in individuals with AS (Clayton-Smith & Laan, 2003).

DON'T FORGET

Although defects on chromosome 15 are responsible for both Prader-Willi syndrome and Angelman syndrome, for PWS, the defect is inherited from the father, while for AS, the defect is passed down by the mother.

Williams Syndrome. A cardiologist from New Zealand, Dr. J. C. P. Williams, is credited with identifying the disorder that bears his name in the early 1960s. In his practice, he found a number of cardiovascular patients who shared similar traits (physical features and cognitive-behavioral patterns). Ultimately, it was discovered that a random mutation on chromosome 7 causes the deletion of ELN, a gene responsible for maintaining heart valves and making blood tissue and other tissues elastic. As a result, individuals with Williams syndrome (WS) are vulnerable to heart problems, and unfortunately many do not live past the age of 50. Physically, in addition to heart problems, infants can be colicky and adolescents are prone to developing diabetes (Bellugi et al., 2007).

In the United States, Dr. Ursula Bellugi and colleagues have been researching WS for several years and have amassed considerable information about the syndrome. The prevalence is rare (1 in 7,500 births), but males with WS have a 50% chance of passing the mutated gene to offspring. Characteristics that have been associated with WS include: hypersensitivity to sound, distinct facial characteristics (elfinlike features, such as puffy eyes, short nose, wide mouth, full cheeks and lips, and small chin), and hypersociability. Bellugi and colleagues (2007) found that children with WS as young as 2 to 3 years of age can have an intense preoccupation with faces. When facial processing occurs in the normal brain, only a specific area of the brain, is activated (fusiform gyrus); however, in the brain of someone with WS, facial recognition activates the majority of the brain's receptive nerve centers Children with WS demonstrate less fear in response to threatening faces, and in at least one study using functional magnetic resonance imaging (fMRI), individuals with WS who were exposed to threatening faces showed less activity than controls in the amydale, which is the area of the brain that regulates the fear response (Meyer-Lindenberg et al., 2005). This may explain tendencies of those with WS to approach strangers without fear.

Intellectually, individuals with WS show strengths verbally but have significant visual-spatial weaknesses. Most present with mild to moderate intellectual deficits. Rourke and colleagues (2002) found many similarities between processing deficits experienced by those with WS and those with nonverbal learning disabilities (NLD) associated with dysfunction in the right hemisphere.

Fragile X Syndrome. The syndrome of Fragile X (FXS) is one of the most common inherited causes of an intellectual disability. Although it was once estimated that 1 in 2,000 males and 1 in 4,000 females have fragile X (Brown et al., 1986), more recent prevalence rates have adjusted the prevalence to 1 in 4,000 males (Turner, Webb, Wake, & Robinson, 1996) and approximately 1 in 6,000 females (nfxf.org). Intellectual levels can vary widely depending on the degree of mutation to the FMR1 gene. Studies have reported normal IQ ratings for at least one male (Merenstein et al., 1993) and one female (Chaste et al., 2012) with fragile X.

Variations in the clinical phenotype are due to changes in the fragile X mental retardation 1 (FMR1 gene, with those receiving only mild changes in gene formation experiencing the least amount of symptoms. Those receiving the most change in the gene develop more severe symptoms of FXS (Reiss & Dant, 2003). Other factors may influence individual characteristics, including such traits as hyperactivity, anxiety, or social deficits that have been genetically transmitted. It has been estimated that up to 60% of men and 20% of women with FXS also have autism (Clifford et al., 2007). Children with FXS who also have comorbid autism present with more severe language problems, social deficits, and lowered IQ than others on the fragile X spectrum (Hagerman, 2002).

DON'T FORGET

Gender effects can make a difference to how socially maladaptive behaviors manifest. While girls with FXS tend to withdraw from social contact, boys with FXS tend to be more aggressive in social situations.

Children born with FXS may exhibit a number of physical, cognitive, and behavioral characteristics along a spectrum of severity, including: physical features (longer ears, faces, and jaws), intellectual deficits, and maladaptive behaviors, such as fearfulness and anxiety (primarily in females) or aggressive and inattentive behaviors (primarily in males) (Hall, De Berndis & Reiss (2006). Freund, Reiss, and Abrams (1993) found that females with FXS demonstrated greater frequency of avoidant disorder and mood disorders compared with control subjects. In addition, ratings by parents and teachers showed greater deficits in the areas of interpersonal socialization skills (girls with FXS were more withdrawn and depressed) than subjects in the control group.

Phenylketonuria. Individuals born with phenylketonuria (PKU) inherit two recessive genes that carry inborn errors of metabolism (IEM). Infants with PKU lack the enzyme phenylalanine hydroxylase, which is needed to produce phenylalanine and is essential to body functioning. Without corrective action, infants with PKU who are exposed to phenylalanine in their diets are at increased risk of intellectual disabilities, since the phenylalanine will continue to build up in their system, eventually reaching toxic levels that can cause damage to the central nervous system (CNS: Koury et al., 2000). The overall prevalence of hyperphenylalaninaemia (HPA/PKU) phenotypes in European populations approximates 1 in 10,000 births (Donlon, Levy, & Scriver, 2004), while estimates for projected births in the United States vary from 1 in 10,000 to 1 in 20,000 births (Resta, 2012). In the United Kingdom, annual prevalence rates for PKU (positive PKU test at birth) is 1/10,000 births (Hardelid et al., 2008). In the United States and Europe, all infants are routinely tested for PKU at birth and are placed on a low phenylalanine diet. Early detection and corrective action will result in normal development and normal intellectual functioning.

Intellectual Disabilities Due to Environmental Toxins (teratogens), Infectious Diseases, or Birth Trauma

As mentioned previously, in addition to chromosomal and genetic etiology, toxins in the environment (referred to as teratogens) can negatively influence development prior to or after birth. During pregnancy, the infant can be exposed to toxins in the uterus, if toxins cross the placenta (which the majority do), potentially causing significant damage, especially if this occurs when vital organs and the nervous system are being formed. After birth, exposure to toxins in the environment (e.g., high levels of lead, mercury) can alter the course of cognitive, physical, and emotional development.

Substance Use/Abuse: Illicit Drugs. With ease of access and the rise of such illegal drugs as crack cocaine, the medical profession was inundated with infants who were born under the influence. By the early 1990s, there was an outcry in the media that something had to be done about the epidemic of crack babies. In their article on the impact of methamphetamine use on infants, Wouldes, Lagasse, Sheridan, and Lester (2004) suggest that although many of the concerns at the time were valid based on research findings that babies exposed to cocaine sustained brain damage and social impairment, many studies conducted at that time were methodologically flawed. Since then, longitudinal studies have addressed these shortcomings, and results now suggest minimal evidence of long-term serious brain damage or impairment (Mayes, Granger, Bornstein, & Zuckerman, 1992). However, even the subtle neurobehavioral patterns and effects that remained were significant (Richardson, Conroy, & Day, 1996). Lester, LaGasse, and Seifer (1998) found that the meaning of these "subtle differences" in school-aged children exposed to cocaine would account for an additional $352 million spent in special education funds.

CAUTION

Trying to isolate the influence of illicit drugs on development is not without its challenges. Because mothers who use illicit drugs are often polydrug users, results of studies often involve the effects of drug interactions rather than any single drug.

Since all illicit drugs cross the placenta, the fetus is vulnerable to whatever toxins are introduced in the system. Studies conducted on rats have suggested many possible areas of compromise developmentally, including impairments in learning, behavior, and motor activity. These changes in the environment in the uterus can contribute to increased risk for physical defects, hemorrhages, and seizures (Espy, Kaufmann, & Glisky, 1999), low birth weight, and potential damage to the central nervous system (Richardson, Hamel, & Goldschmidt, 1996).

Most studies of the effects of drugs on the developing child focus on behavior shortly after birth or during early childhood, so little is known about the long-term effects. Finally, growing up in an environment where drugs continue to be used can often mean growing up in a climate of chaos, stress, poverty, lack of stability, poor monitoring, poor nutrition, and possibly multiple caregivers. Given this complex mix, it is not difficult to see how it would be a challenge to make causative links to specific factors. However, a longitudinal study out of Sweden may shed some light on some of the outcomes of illicit drug exposure on child development. In this series of studies, 65 Swedish children who were exposed to amphetamines were tracked from birth to adolescence. Initial findings were that girls were especially influenced in their physical growth and tended to be shorter and weigh less than their peers not exposed to drugs—a characteristic that remained stable at least until preadolescence (Cernerud, Eriksson, Jonsson, Steneroth, & Zetterstrom 1996). A follow-up of behavioral and social adjustment found that increased duration and amount of drug exposure was related to increased behavioral problems (aggression) and social maladjustment (Billing et al., 1994).

> # CAUTION
> ....
> Results remain mixed regarding the impact of drugs on cognitive development. Although research does support problems with intellectual development in some children exposed to alcohol during pregnancy (Nanson & Hiscock, 1990), according to Behnke et al. (2013), "to date limited data are available revealing an association between prenatal methamphetamine exposure and IQ" (p. 1015).

Fetal Alcohol Syndrome. Mothers who drink alcohol during pregnancy risk giving birth to an infant with fetal alcohol syndrome (FAS) or fetal alcohol effects (FAE). The difference between the two conditions is that while those with FAS can have the full-blown array of possible symptoms, those who have FAE experience a lesser form of the condition, likely due to the consumption of less alcohol by the mother during pregnancy (Streissguth, Bookstein, & Barr, 2004a). Connor, Sampson, Bookstein, Barr, and Streissguth (2000) found that those with FAE had a mean IQ score of 90 while those with FAS only had an average IQ score of 79. There has been some controversy as to how to best define and distinguish among the various forms of FAS, which more recently has also been referred to as fetal alcohol spectrum disorder (FASD). FASD is defined as "the spectrum of structural anomalies and behavioral and neurocognitive disabilities" that can present in those who have been exposed to alcohol during pregnancy (Hoyme et al., 2005, p. 39). Although individuals who have the more severe forms of FAS are more readily identified, individuals with milder forms of the syndrome may go undiagnosed and untreated (Little, Snell, Rosenfield, Gilstrap & Gant, 1990). There is discontent among many clinicians and researchers regarding the use of the term FAE, since this description applies to such a wide variety of possible symptoms that it is of minimal value for diagnostic purposes (Anase, Jones & Clarren, 1996).

It has been estimated that one-third of all babies born to mothers who consume alcohol during pregnancy will develop FAS (Streissguth et al., 2004b). There are several characteristics of FAS that have been documented in research, including CNS dysfunction, which may present as intellectual disability, irritability and/or hyperactivity, and impairments in motor functioning involving coordination and overactivity (Connor, Sampson, & Bookstein, 2001). There may be distinct physical features, such as a small head, underdeveloped upper lip, and widely spaced eyes, which may become less noticeable over time. However, deficits in the cognitive areas as well as impaired motor coordination and hyperactivity seem to be evident and persist over the course of time (Schonfeld, Mattson, & Lang, 2001).

In addition to broad cognitive deficits that are associated with intellectual disability, individuals with FASD also show more specific problems with the executive functions responsible for cognitive flexibility, planning, and organizing information. Particular areas of weakness for those with FAS include the ability to shift (change strategies) and an inability to detect subtle cues (such as social cues), both of which can significantly hinder success developmentally (Connor et al., 2000). Streissguth and colleagues (2004) found that children with FASD require more support for academics, with 42% of their sample having a placement in special education and 66% receiving resource room assistance, while 65% were receiving remedial support. In this sample of 415 students, the greatest areas of deficit were evident on the Vineland Adaptive Behavior Scales and their performance on arithmetic. Individuals with FASD are at increased risk of becoming involved with the juvenile justice system (Streissguth et al., 2004) due to their ongoing problems in areas of intellectual disability, learning disabilities, attention, and social problems. The Substance Abuse and Mental Health Services Administration (SAMSHA, 2007) has recommended that youth who come in contact with juvenile justice be screened for FASD, since those with the syndrome are at increased risk for breaking the law due to their vulnerability to peer pressure, lack of consideration of the consequences of their behavior, and poor sense of personal boundaries.

Lead-Based Paint. Although lead-based paint has been banned in the United States since 1978, in their study of housing across the United States, Clickner et al. (2002) "estimated 25% of the nation's housing (equivalent to 24 million housing units) had significant lead-based paint hazards in the form of deteriorated paint, dust lead, or bare soil lead" with 1.2 million units housing low-income families with children under 6 years of age (p. 603). The Committee on Environmental Health (CEH, 2005) states that the effects of lead-based paint on the CNS are the most common reported outcome, with impairment in IQ being the effect most studied. Studies have demonstrated that blood lead concentration is associated with lower IQ scores, and this has been identified as young as 5 years of age (Pocock, Smith, & Baghurst, 1994). The Centers for Disease Control and Prevention (CDC) suggests that lead-blood concentration levels of 10 μg/dL or more represent cause for concern (CEH, 2005). However, some studies suggest that blood levels below that level can also be detrimental to IQ (Canfield et al., 2003). Prenatal exposure to lead-based paint has been implicated in the development of brain damage and myriad physical side effects (Davis, Change, Burns, Robinson, & Dossett, 2004). Other areas that have been related to exposure to lead-based paint, include attention, memory, learning, behavior, and school performance (Davis et al., 2004).

Rubella. The risk for the fetus acquiring congenital rubella (German measles) syndrome is 50% if the mother is exposed to rubella during the embryonic period (3 to 8 weeks' gestation). During this time, important vital organs are being formed, and rubella has been known to cause significant potential damage during this period. Impairments can range from defects in the formation of the sensory organs (eye, ear), mental functioning, and inner organs or the heart (Eberhart-Phillips, Frederick, Baron, & Mascola, 1993). Because congenital rubella syndrome involves exposure to rubella in utero, damage often takes the form of birth defects. Children who have congenital rubella syndrome often experience multiple handicaps, including sensory impairments (hearing loss) and intellectual disabilities, and are prone to demonstrating self-injurious behaviors (SIBs) or aggressive behaviors (Carvill & Marston, 2002).

Birth Trauma. Complicated deliveries can result in a deprivation of oxygen (anoxia), which can potentially cause deficits in intellectual functioning.

Health and Injuries. Children can also experience reduced cognitive/ intellectual capacity due to acquired head injuries, severe nutritional deprivation or developing encephalitis or meningitis.

DIFFERENTIAL DIAGNOSES

The fifth edition of the *Diagnostic and Statistical Manual of Mental Disorders* (*DSM–5*) classifies an intellectual disability as a neurodevelopmental disorder that has onset during the developmental period. As such, the disorder shares similar features with a number of other disorders that are characterized by "developmental deficits that produce impairments of personal, social, academic, or occupational functioning." The nature of the deficits in this category can range from "very specific" limitations that can be evident in such areas as learning or executive functions, to more pervasive problems in areas such as social skills or intellectual/cognitive functioning (APA), 2013, p. 31). Furthermore, the *DSM–5* emphasizes that disorders in this category, can often co-occur, such as an intellectual disability, autism spectrum disorder (ASD), learning disorders, and attention-deficit/hyperactivity disorder (ADHD). Therefore, when diagnosing an intellectual disability, not only is it important to look for potential comorbid disorders that may be present, it is equally important to engage in differential diagnosis to rule out potential diagnoses in favor of a diagnosis of an intellectual disability. The *DSM–5* states that an intellectual disability is a neurodevelopmental disorder distinct from *neurocognitive disorders* that is "characterized by a loss of cognitive functioning"; however, individuals can be diagnosed with both an intellectual disability and a neurocognitive disorder, such as an individual who has Down syndrome but also develops *Alzheimer's disorder* later in life or an individual with an intellectual disability who may also suffer from a neurocognitive disorder resulting from a *traumatic brain injury* (TBI; APA, 2013). Individuals with an intellectual disability can also be distinguished from individuals who have other neurocognitive disorders, such as *communication disorders* or *specific learning disorders*, since those disorders do not include deficits in intellectual ability or adaptive behavior. However, it is possible to be diagnosed with both an intellectual disability and communication or specific learning disorders if an individual meets the full criteria for both disorders. The *DSM–5* also recognizes that individuals who have autism spectrum disorder often also meet criteria for an intellectual disability and APA (2013) cautions that in these individuals assessment of intellectual functioning is imperative and should be re-assessed, since results can be unstable during the early childhood period.

COMORBIDITY

The *DSM–5* states that the risk of co-occurring "mental, neurodevelopmental, medical and physical conditions" (e.g., cerebral palsy, epilepsy) can be three to four times higher in individuals with intellectual disabilities than in the population at large, with the most common comorbid disorders being: "attention deficit/hyperactivity disorder; depressive and bipolar disorders; anxiety disorders; autism spectrum disorders; stereotypic movement disorder (with or without self-injurious behavior) impulse control disorders; and major neurocognitive disorder" (APA, 2013, p. 40).

DON'T FORGET

In a study of 474 randomly selected children (ages 7 to 20 years) from Dutch schools for the intellectually disabled, Dekker and Koot (2003) found that 21.9% of the children met criteria for anxiety disorder, 4.4% for mood disorder, and 25.1% for disruptive behavior disorder. The staggering statistic from this study was that less than one-third of those with a psychiatric disorder (27%) received any assistance from mental health care the previous year.

Emerson (2003) investigated the prevalence of psychiatric disorders in children—with and without a diagnosis of an intellectual disability—in a sample of 438 children (age 5 to 15 years) living in Wales, England, and Scotland. The prevalence of conduct disorder, anxiety disorder, hyperkinesis, and pervasive developmental disorder was significantly greater among children with an intellectual disability than their peers without a diagnosis of an intellectual disability. In the sample of children with an intellectual disability, the prevalence rate for meeting diagnostic criteria for any disorder was 39% compared to 8.1% for peers without a diagnosis of an intellectual disability. There was no statistical difference in the prevalence rate for depressive disorders, eating disorders, or psychotic disorders in children with or without a diagnosis of an intellectual disability.

🔊 TEST YOURSELF 🔊

1. **At the time of the publication of their book on genetics and public health, Khoury et al. (2000) noted that _____ genes had been identified that could increase the risk of having an intellectual disability:**
   (a) 579
   (b) 1,010
   (c) 872
   (d) 650

2. **The risk of having a child with Down syndrome for a female in her mid-30s is:**
   (a) 1 in 200
   (b) 1 in 800
   (c) 1 in 2,000
   (d) 1 in 500

3. **Children with Prader-Willi syndrome inherit a defect on chromosome ____ passed on by the _____.**
   (a) 15, mother
   (b) 21, mother
   (c) 15, father
   (d) 21, father

4. **All of the following are true regarding individuals with Williams syndrome except that they:**
   (a) are hypersocial.
   (b) are vulnerable to cardiac problems.
   (c) have a heightened response in the amygdale to threatening faces.
   (d) have a mutation (deletion of ELN) on chromosome 7.

5. **A female diagnosed with fragile X syndrome (FXS) is more likely to be:**
   (a) socially withdrawn.
   (b) socially aggressive.
   (c) hypersocial.
   (d) prone to laughing at inappropriate times.

6. **In the United Kingdom, what is the annual prevalence rate for infants who test positive for PKU:**
   (a) 1/ 10,000 births
   (b) 1/ 20,000 births
   (c) 1/ 5,000 births
   (d) 1/ 25,000 births

7. **Of all the children born to mothers who consume alcohol, what percentage is likely to meet criteria for a diagnosis of fetal alcohol syndrome (FAS)?**
   (a) 66%
   (b) 25%
   (c) 33%
   (d) 50%

8. **Which of the following is true regarding exposure to rubella during pregnancy?**
   (a) 50% of mothers exposed to rubella risk carrying an infant who will develop congenital rubella syndrome.
   (b) Congenital rubella syndrome can result in birth defects involving the sensory organs, such as hearing loss.
   (c) Congenital rubella syndrome can result in the development of an intellectual disability and aggressive behaviors.
   (d) All of the above.

Answers: 1. c; 2. b; 3. c; 4. c; 5. a; 6. d; 7. c; 8. d.

Three

CURRENT INTELLECTUAL DISABILITY DIAGNOSTIC AND FEDERAL EDUCATION CRITERIA

This chapter provides an overview of the nature of systems of classification involved in a diagnosis of an intellectual disability (ID). In this book, discussion of the diagnostic criteria is based on the new *Diagnostic and Statistical Manual of Mental Disorders, Fifth Edition* (*DSM–5*; American Psychiatric Association [APA], 2013) and the Individuals with Disabilities Education Improvement Act of 2004 (IDEA 2004). The chapter also addresses important changes in the way we conceptualize intellectual disabilities resulting from shifts in perspectives on the disorder under the influences of the American Association on Intellectual and Developmental Disabilities (AAIDD). The chapter will take the perspective that there are two important goals of assessment: (1) determining whether symptoms meet criteria for an intellectual disability and how this is conceptualized by the different classification systems, and (2) the need for assessment to inform treatment and interventions. Since assessment also provides significant information regarding differential diagnoses–or whether symptoms indicate a different disorder but one that shares similar features—it is also essential to provide information on the most common disorders/problems that present with symptoms similar to an intellectual disability (e.g., autism spectrum disorder, reactive attachment disorder, developmental delay, lack of early stimulation, and learning disabilities such as dyslexia, in order to ensure that the disorder is appropriately identified.

THE DSM–5

As was previously discussed in Chapter 1, the criteria for intellectual disability has evolved over the course of *DSM* revisions based on how the disorder has been conceptualized. In the current manual, the *DSM–5* (APA, 2013), an intellectual disability is considered to be one of the neurodevelopmental disorders which houses disorders that have onset during the developmental period and are characterized by "developmental deficits that produce impairments of personal, social, academic or occupational functioning" (p. 31). An intellectual disability shares many features with other disorders within this group, including: communication disorders (language disorder, speech sound disorder, childhood-onset fluency disorder, social communication disorder), autism spectrum disorder (ASD), attention-deficit/hyperactivity disorder (ADHD), specific learning disorders, and motor disorders (developmental coordination disorder, stereotypic movement disorder, tic disorders).

Although an intellectual disability shares features similar to other disorders within the same category, it is the emphasis on deficits in general mental abilities that set the disorder apart from the other disorders mentioned. These deficits can result in impaired functioning in several possible areas, such as: reasoning, abstract thinking, planning, judgment, and the acquisition of information in such areas as learning academics or profiting from life's experiences. Often thinking is very concrete, and they are often limited in how much they can generalize information from one set of circumstances to another.

The *DSM–5* describes an intellectual disability as a "disorder with onset during the developmental period that includes both intellectual and adaptive functioning deficits in conceptual, social and practical domains" (APA, 2013, p. 33). A diagnosis of an intellectual disability involves meeting three specific criteria:

- Intellectual deficits in areas that impact an ability to learn (academically) or profit from experiences, such as impairments in abstract reasoning, planning, organizing, judgment, and thinking, which are documented through "clinical assessment and individualized, standardized intelligence testing." The *DSM–5*, maintains that the standard score cutoff for intellectual functioning to meet criteria for an intellectual disability is an IQ score of 70 (plus or minus 5 to account for measurement error), which is the same IQ criteria that was stated in the previous version of the *DSM* (DSM-IV, TR) APA, 2000). The IQ cutoff of 70 is based on the rationale that this represents a deficit of 2 standard deviations below the mean (e.g., 30-point discrepancy from an average IQ of 100).
- Adaptive functioning deficits resulting in an inability to achieve age-appropriate and sociocultural standards that would allow for an individual to obtain sufficient levels of personal independence and social responsibility. The areas impacted by adaptive functioning deficits include one or more activities of day-to-day living, such as social engagement, communication, and independent living, and can impact a wide variety of circumstances, such as one's home life, school, work, and community involvement.

- Onset of the above two criteria (intellectual and adaptive deficits) occur during the developmental period.

In addition to these three criteria, the *DSM* also provides a set of specifiers that can be used to indicate the severity of the disorder, based on the degree of deficits evident in adaptive functioning: *mild, moderate, severe,* and *profound.*

Specifiers

Since there is a wide range of variability in how the disorder may present in different individuals, the *DSM* encourages the use of four different specifiers to indicate an individual's level of adaptive functioning in three different domain areas: *conceptual domain, social domain,* and *practical domain.* The severity levels and their descriptions can be seen in **Rapid Reference** 3.1.

DON'T FORGET

Up until the fourth revision of the *DSM—DSM–IV–TR* (APA, 2000), the specifiers of mild, moderate, severe, and profound were used to refer to levels of intellectual functioning. However, with the advent of the *DSM–5* (APA, 2013), these specifiers no longer refer to intellectual functioning but instead refer to the level of intensity of services required due to deficits in adaptive functioning.

≡ Rapid Reference 3.1 Specifiers and Severity Levels for Adaptive Functioning

Severity	Conceptual Domain	Social Domain	Practical Domain
Mild	Differences may not be evident in very young children, but by school age delays may be evident in acquiring core academic skills, while adults will likely experience problems with organization, money management, and other activities relying on functional academics.	Social engagement and communication may be delayed. Children may not interpret subtle social cues or recognize risky situations. Emotion and behavior regulation may be problematic.	May manage activities like self-care, recreational outlets, and a job that is highly structured. Support may be needed to manage legal and financial affairs or making important decisions (e.g., health care).

Severity	Conceptual Domain	Social Domain	Practical Domain
Moderate	Deficits may be evident in language development, and increased supports may be needed to enhance academic skills, especially in areas requiring reasoning involving money or time. In adulthood, academics may plateau at an elementary level and supports will be needed to manage day-to-day functioning.	Language delays and immature social skills may interfere with success in making and keeping friendships. In adulthood, caregivers are needed to provide ongoing support for decision making in day-to-day situations.	Self-care can be acquired successfully through training and practice, although it may need monitoring. Job success will require considerable support from coworkers and management. If maladaptive behaviors exist, social problems may result.
Severe	Limited understanding of concepts such as time, money, or numbers. Require ongoing support	Speech is often limited, and speech augmentation may be required. May be able to communicate using simple speech and gestures.	Support and supervision required for all activities of self-care and daily living. Some may exhibit maladaptive and self-injurious behaviors.
Profound	Often accompanied by comorbid motor and sensory impairments. there is limited ability to comprehend written or spoken language. Extensive support required.	Comorbid motor and sensory impairments also make social engagement challenging. Very limited ability to understand speech or gestures. They require extensive support.	Due to the complex nature of accompanying comorbid impairments, these individuals require extensive support.

Source: Adapted from the American Psychiatric Association (2013), *Diagnostic and Statistical Manual of Mental Disorders*, 5th ed. (pp. 34–36).

Global Developmental Delay

In addition to changing how the disorder is conceptualized to more closely align with how the disorder is perceived by the American Association on Intellectual and Developmental Disabilities (AAIDD), the *DSM–5* also included a new diagnosis which aligns more closely with the educational classification system (IDEA 2004), in the introduction of the diagnosis of global developmental delay. This special category is reserved for individuals under the age of 5 years who may be suspected of having an intellectual disability but cannot be assessed due to circumstances (e.g., child is too young). In this special case, the diagnosis will be given if the child does not achieve age-appropriate developmental milestones in several areas of intellectual functioning; however, this is a temporary diagnosis and is only valid for a period of time until arrangements can be made for a full clinical assessment.

Unspecified Intellectual Disability

The *DSM–5* also added another category of diagnosis—"unspecified intellectual disability" for children "over the age of 5 years who cannot be assessed due to challenges, such as impairments in sensory functions (blindness, deafness) motor functions or severe behavior problems." Similar to global developmental delay, this is also considered a temporary diagnosis that should be replaced once assessment is conducted.

AMERICAN ASSOCIATION ON INTELLECTUAL AND DEVELOPMENTAL DISABILITIES

In 2007, the American Association on Mental Retardation (AAMR) changed its name to the American Association on Intellectual and Developmental Disabilities (AAIDD) to reflect the changing conceptualization of the disorder, which has now been recognized internationally as "intellectual disability" or "intellectual developmental disorder" (as it is recognized in the *International Code of Diseases* [*ICD–10*]; WHO, 1992). The AAIDD recognizes the same three diagnostic criteria as the *DSM–5*, involving: IQ cutoff for intellectual disability (70, plus or minus 5), adaptive deficits, and onset in the developmental period. However, there continue to be differences between the two categorical systems. Whereas the *DSM–5* relies on specifiers to reflect the degree of supports required in three areas of adaptive functioning (conceptual, social, and pragmatic), the AAIDD profiles four subtypes of intellectual disabilities, based on the degree of support services required: intermittent, limited, extensive, or pervasive (Shalock et al., 2009). Once a diagnosis of an intellectual disability is made, it is the goal of AAIDD that emphasis be placed on the planning of supports that will reduce the gap between an individual's capabilities and his or her skills to promote a successful lifestyle. The latest definition of intellectual disability is found in the 11th edition of the *AAIDD Definition Manual* (AAIDD, 2010).

While AAIDD supports an IQ cutoff score similar to that suggested by the *DSM–5*; it also advocates for an IQ level that could potentially raise the cutoff to 76. In an interview which can be accessed on the AAIDD website (http://aaidd.org), Robert Schalock discusses how the association has changed its view on intellectual disabilities and how the association has "continually grappled with the issue of IQ." In discussing the concepts of cutoff score and standard error of measurement, Schalock makes the point that in itself, rather than use a cutoff of 70, it is possible that the definition may also include those with an IQ of 75.

The goal in the latest *AAIDD Definition Manual* (AAIDD, 2010) is not just to clarify a definition of what an intellectual disability is but to provide a "supports-based definition" that includes addressing the critical role that a support system can play in maximizing success. In discussing the importance of the latest definition, AAIDD states that it is important to understand the assumptions that underlie a definition. In this regard he outlines five assumptions that support the definition as it now stands, with the final two assumptions directly related to the role of support systems. The following five assumptions are taken verbatim from that interview:

- Limitations in present functioning must be considered within the context of community environments typical of the individual's age peers and culture. This assumption contextualizes the term "intellectual disability."
- Valid assessment considers cultural and linguistic diversity as well as differences in communication, sensory, motor, and behavioral factors.
- Within an individual, limitations often coexist with strengths.
- An important purpose of describing limitations is to develop a profile of needed supports. This assumption is so critical because very often people just make a diagnosis and this ends the process. What we stress is that the diagnostic process must include the planning of individual supports as a key part of that process.
- With appropriate personalized supports over a sustained period, the life functioning of a person with intellectual disability generally will improve. I think the importance of this assumption is self-evident. This assumption results in the need to consider the whole individual and not just the person's limitations. The intent of personalized supports is to enhance the level of human functioning.

As is evident from these assumptions, the committee that developed the definition had a working model that built on previous definitions and focused on how to best incorporate systems of support within the definition itself. As a result, the definition and classification of an intellectual disability by the AAIDD emphasizes the interaction that exists between an individual's capacities and the environment in which the individual lives, works, or learns, with the goal being to reduce the gap between the capabilities and the environmental demands, or demands of the "contexts" in which the individual lives (AAIDD, 2010). AAIDD identifies "context" as one of the five factors that influence the degree to which an individual is able to maximize his or her ability to function. The other four factors include: intellectual abilities, adaptive behavior, health, and participation (AAIDD, 2010).

Intensity of Supports

When the American Association on Mental Retardation (AAMR) published their *Definition and Classification Manual* in (1992) it was the beginning of a journey that would last several years in their quest to determine how to best meet an individual's needs based on the context in which he or she was living, in order to promote the highest level of human functioning. As a result, Thompson and colleagues (2002) put forth the recommendation that there was a need for a scale to document the nature and extent of supports that would be required to increase an individual's quality of life and independent living. Following up on this recommendation, a task force was appointed to develop an instrument to fulfill this need.

The resulting instrument, the Supports Intensity Scale (SIS; Thompson et al., 2004), contains six subscales designed to measure the nature and intensity of needs in 49 different areas. The six subscales include: i) home living, ii) community living, iii) lifelong learning, iv) employment, v) health and safety, and vi) social. In addition, the scale also includes sections on issues of protection and advocacy as well as potential behavioral and medical concerns. There have been several studies that have investigated the validity of these scales. Wehmeyer and colleagues (2009) investigated the SIS's ability to detect support needs in a population of 272 adults with an intellectual disability and related disabilities. Results of that study revealed that use of the SIS was significantly related to meeting needs of those studied and predicted higher levels of needed supports.

Wehmeyer, Tasse, Davies, and Stock (2012) investigated the potential role of technology in serving the needs of individuals with an intellectual disability along a continuum of severity (mild, moderate, severe, and profound), and comorbid conditions (e.g., autism, physical disabilities, psychiatric disabilities). As would be anticipated, individuals with a mild intellectual disability evidenced the lowest intensity of support needs, followed by those with a moderate intellectual disability, comorbid psychiatric disorders, and comorbid intellectual disability and autism. Individuals with a severe and profound intellectual disability and those with comorbid intellectual disability and physical impairments demonstrated the highest levels of intensity of support needs. With the exception of those with severe and profound intellectual disabilities, support for needs in the area of lifelong learning was the greatest for all groups. To this end, the authors discuss the potential role of technology in supporting these needs for individuals with an intellectual disability.

INDIVIDUALS WITH DISABILITIES EDUCATION IMPROVEMENT ACT OF 2004

The Individuals with Disabilities Education Improvement Act (IDEA 2004) was last reauthorized by Congress in November 2004, with the passing of IDEA 2004, which President George W. Bush signed into law on December 3, 2004. The law has been changed a number of times, with more regulations and procedures added with each successive change. Prior to 2004, the act was last revised in 1997. In the following discussion, we include the section numbers (such as Sec. 614) to indicate which portion of the law we are addressing so that readers can retrieve those sections in their entirety if needed.

IDEA 2004 is a federal law that was developed to protect the rights of students with disabilities. Within the law, a disability is defined as "a natural part of the human experience" (Sec. 601). The goal of IDEA 2004 is to equalize educational opportunities for individuals with disabilities. IDEA 2004 lists

DON'T FORGET

The entire contents of the IDEA 2004 congressional report can be accessed at http://idea.ed.gov/.

13 specific categories of disabilities children may experience that are mandated under the act, including children who have the following needs:

(a) Individuals have one of the 13 disabilities: intellectual disability, hearing impairments (including deafness), speech or language impairments, visual impairments (including blindness), serious emotional disturbance (hereinafter referred to as emotional disturbance), orthopedic impairments, autism, traumatic brain injury, other health impairments (which includes attention deficit disorder), or specific learning disabilities.

(b) The disability interferes with their ability to learn, and they require special education and related services as a result of their disability.

In addition to these 13 categories of disabilities, IDEA 2004 also states that at the discretion of the state and the school district, children ages 3 through 9 (or any subset of that age range, including ages 3 through 5) may also receive special education and related services if the child is experiencing developmental delays. However, it is important to know that under IDEA 2004, states are not mandated to provide services for children with developmental delays, and if they choose to provide these services, they may select a more limited age span to service. We discuss this at greater length when we focus on how the act applies to school-age children (Part B of IDEA 2004).

The major goal of IDEA 2004 is to improve educational opportunities for children with disabilities to ensure that they have the same opportunities for participation, independent living, and economic self-sufficiency as their peers without disabilities. We include parts of IDEA 2004 that especially refer to how an individual with an intellectual disability may qualify for services under IDEA, although the entire act does refer to all children with disabilities. Specifically, the legislation strives to:

- Ensure that children with disabilities have access to a free appropriate public education (FAPE). This includes special education and related services (e.g., counseling, speech and physical therapy, etc.) when these services are required to address the child's individual learning needs.
- Ensure that undiagnosed disabilities do not prevent children from obtaining a successful educational experience.
- Ensure that public schools provide the necessary services for children with disabilities to have a FAPE.
- Protect the rights of children with disabilities and their parents. (Each state/district must develop a set of Procedural Safeguards.)
- Ensure that funds are available to support states, local school districts, and agencies to provide special education and related services.
- Monitor the effectiveness of educational programs in meeting the needs of children with disabilities.

The law is divided into four major sections:

- *Parts A and B.* These sections cover eligibility procedures, regulations, and required services for children between the ages of 3 years and 21 years.
- *Part C.* This section of the law pertains to services for infants and toddlers with disabilities, under 3 years of age.
- *Part D.* The final section discusses national activities that have been promoted to enhance educational services for children with disabilities.

DON'T FORGET

Under IDEA 2004, infants and toddlers with disabilities and developmental delays can receive *intervention services* as part of their individualized family service plan (IFSP). Also, children with disabilities between the ages of 3 and 21 can receive *special education and related services* as part of their *individualized education program (IEP)*.

Similar to the emphasis on "contexts" found in the definition of an intellectual disability according to AAIDD, IDEA 2004 also stressed the context in which learning takes place and that improving educational success for children with disabilities can only be achieved in an environment that supports:

- High expectations for success and meeting developmental goals with maximum access to the general curriculum.
- Increased parent participation in a child's educational program.
- Coordinating efforts of IDEA 2004 with other educational laws, such as the Elementary and Secondary Education Act of 1965 (ESEA), as amended by the No Child Left Behind Act of 2001 (NCLB), to increase the emphasis on children with disabilities having the same opportunities for education as their peers without disabilities. IDEA 2004 includes more than 60 references to ESEA/NCLB, importing terms directly from these laws. For example, IDEA makes references to achievement in the "core academic subjects"; discusses qualifications for special education teachers related to standards for "highly qualified teachers" noted in NCLB; and discusses provisions for "homeless children," which were not cited in previous versions of IDEA.
- The regular curriculum with special education and related services when required.
- The use and development of technology to maximize access to education.
- Increased effort to reduce mislabeling and high dropout rates of minority children with disabilities. IDEA 2004 mandates states to develop policies and procedures to minimize the overidentification of students from racially and ethnically diverse cultures.

IDEA 2004: Part C—The Infants and Toddlers with Disabilities Program (Ages Birth to 2)

IDEA 2004 addresses intervention services for children from birth to the end of the child's second year. Under *Part C of IDEA 2004 (Sec. 631)*, financial assistance is provided to each state to:

- Develop multidisciplinary, interagency systems to provide early intervention services for infants and toddlers with disabilities and their families.
- Encourage expansion of opportunities for children under 3 years of age who would be at risk of having substantial developmental delay if they did not receive early intervention services.
- Identify, evaluate, and meet the needs of all children, particularly minority, low-income, inner city, and rural children, and infants and toddlers in foster care.

According to IDEA 2004, *early intervention services* include those services that may be required to assist in the identification and remediation of problems for infants and toddlers with identified developmental delays or may offer services to those at risk of developmental delays that could have a negative influence on a child's ability to learn. IDEA 2004 uses the term "at-risk infant or toddler" to refer to a child under 3 years of age who would be at risk of being substantially delayed if early intervention services were not provided. IDEA uses the term "developmental delay" (Sec. 635) to refer to a delay of:

- 35% or more in one of the developmental areas which will be discussed shortly, or
- 25% or more in two or more of the developmental areas.

Delays (Sec. 632) may be evident in one of five developmental areas:

1. How the child learns (cognitive development)
2. Physical development (motor skills)
3. Communication skills (speech and language development)
4. Social or emotional development
5. Adaptive functioning (daily living and self-help skills)

CAUTION

It is important to remember that a developmental delay is conceptualized as a "lag" in development, where milestones are delayed but can develop at some later time (i.e., the *child can catch up*), if given the appropriate interventions. A delay differs from a "deficit" in that an individual with a deficit will need to have modifications to their environment to accommodate the deficit.

Congress has allocated funds to help states develop early intervention services. States can use these funds to develop programs for children who are at risk of developing disabilities. For children under 3 years of age, services can be provided by several different agencies. In some states, the department of education may be responsible for programs for children of all ages; however, in other states, other agencies, such as the health department, may be responsible for programs designed for infants and toddlers. When multiple agencies are involved, a lead agency is established, and a service coordinator is selected from that agency to oversee the intervention services.

IDEA 2004 stresses the importance of developing an effective transition plan to assist in providing a smooth and effective transition from interventions covered under Part C (Infants and Toddlers with Disabilities) to preschool

DON'T FORGET

Developmental delay in the IDEA 2004 context is very similar to what the *DSM–5* refers to as "global developmental delay." Remember, the *DSM–5* states that this temporary diagnostic term is reserved for children under 5 years of age who do not meet developmental milestones but whose clinical severity level cannot be determined since standardized testing is not available (e.g., due to child's age).

programs existing under Part B (Education of All Children with Disabilities). IDEA 2004 mandates that by the child's third birthday, an individualized education program (IEP), or an individualized family service plan (IFSP) must be developed and implemented.

DON'T FORGET

Under IDEA 2004, infants and toddlers with disabilities and developmental delays who are eligible for services can receive intervention programs designed to target specific areas of delay: physical, cognitive, speech and language (communication), social, emotional/behavioral, and adaptive functioning.

IDEA 2004: Part B—Special Education Programs and Services: Preschool (Age 3 to 5)

Under Part B of IDEA 2004, all public schools must provide free special education services for eligible children with disabilities once the child turns 3 years of age. With the introduction of IDEA 2004, special education preschool programs were mandated for eligible children with disabilities who were between 3 and 5 years of age.

DON'T FORGET

According to IDEA 2004, children can become eligible for special education services if they meet the following three criteria:

1. They have received an individual evaluation (as set out in the regulations).
2. The evaluation has confirmed the existence of a disability (in one of 13 specified areas).
3. The disability interferes with the child's ability to learn.

Children with Developmental Delays. Prior to the 1997 reauthorization of IDEA, the law stipulated that preschool-age children (3 to 5 years of age) who demonstrated *developmental delays* could be eligible for special education services if the child demonstrated significant developmental delays determined through a comprehensive initial evaluation. However, the developmental delay classification was to be removed prior to the child's sixth birthday. At that time, further evaluation would be conducted to determine whether the child would continue to receive services under one or more of the 13 categories of disabilities or whether the child no longer eligible to receive services under IDEA.

When IDEA was reauthorized in 1997, the age range for consideration of developmental delay was expanded from 3 to 5 years to the age range of 3 through 9 years. Under IDEA 2004, this expanded age range of 3 through 9 is retained, and now the term "including the subset of ages 3 through 5" has been added to the age description. Children with identified delays in one of the five developmental areas—physical development, cognitive development, communication development, social or emotional development, or adaptive development—may be granted access to special education and related services, at the discretion of the state, if these services are deemed necessary. However, as noted previously, IDEA 2004 did not change the discretionary nature of this service, and states are not mandated to provide special education and related services for children with developmental delays.

The controversy regarding whether the expanded age should be adopted has resulted in wide variations in age criteria for the developmental delay category among the states. Proponents in favor of extending the age of classification believe that standardized tests are not as reliable in early childhood and could possibly lead to misdiagnosis. Furthermore, the need to have children meet criteria for one of the 13 disability categories might lead to inappropriate diagnoses or ineligibility for services at a time when increased services might have the most impact. Those who are not in favor of increasing the age span are concerned with the overidentification of children eligible for special education services.

Special Education Services for School-Age Children (Ages 3 to 21). Special education and related services (such as special transportation, speech and language services, assistive technology) must be available from the child's third birthday until receipt of a high school diploma or the end of the school year of the student's 21st birthday, whichever is earlier.

Under IDEA 2004 (Sec. 614), the school district shall conduct a full and individual initial evaluation to determine whether a child meets eligibility criteria for special education and related services. IDEA 2004 notes that requests for an initial evaluation can be made by either a parent of a child, a state department of education or other state agency, or the school district.

Special education instruction can also be provided in the home, hospitals, or alternative settings. School districts are responsible for providing a continuum of special education placements that adhere to a policy of offering the least restrictive environment (LRE) ranging from minimal services (such as 20 minutes weekly) to full-time placement in an alternative setting.

> **DON'T FORGET**
> ....
> If a child 3 through 21 years of age has a disability that is interfering with their ability to learn, he or she is entitled to a *free appropriate public education* (FAPE) in the *least restrictive environment* (LRE).

> **DON'T FORGET**
> ....
> You can find a list of each state's department of special education in **Appendix A**.

Transition Planning. Transitions between schools and programs can be stressful for all children. However, for children with intellectual and developmental disabilities, transitions can be especially challenging. With the advent of IDEA 2004, transition planning for students with disabilities has been increasingly emphasized and focuses on key transition periods: transition services when a child turns 3 and transition services when a child turns 16.

IDEA 2004 emphasizes the need to have an effective transition plan in place in order to provide a smooth transition from interventions provided under Part C (infants and toddlers) of IDEA to those available in Part B (3 through 21 years of age). As a result, IDEA 2004 mandates that an IEP or an IFSP must be developed and implemented prior to a child's third birthday.

For adolescents, significant focus has been placed on the transition planning, which is extremely important for individuals with an intellectual disability. Often these individuals will have multiple needs that are serviced by different organizations as they progress from secondary education to prepare them for further education, employment, and independent living. Further discussion about transitions from secondary school will be addressed in Chapter 8, *Post Assessment Planning*.

DIFFERENTIAL DIAGNOSES AND COMORBID CONDITIONS

In this section, we discuss some of the most common disorders/problems that present with symptoms similar to an intellectual disability or that can co-occur with an intellectual disability (e.g., autism spectrum disorder, reactive attachment disorder, developmental delay, lack of early stimulation, and learning disabilities (such as dyslexia).

Autism Spectrum Disorder

Using criteria from the *DSM–IV–TR* (APA, 2000), it was estimated that 75% of those diagnosed with autism would also meet criteria for an intellectual disability. However, criteria for autism spectrum disorder (ASD have changed from previous criteria used to diagnose autism when it was considered to be one of the pervasive developmental disorders (PDD). Current criteria in the *DSM-5* (APA, 2013) recognize two fundamental areas that are characterized by:

- Qualitative and persistent impairment in social interaction and communication (three symptoms indicating deficits in: social reciprocity, nonverbal communication, and maintaining and developing social interaction); and
- Restricted, repetitive patterns of behaviors/activities (two symptoms from a list of repetitive, stereotypical, and nonfunctional activities, or hyper- or hypo-reactivity) (APA, 2013, p. 50).

While a large number of individuals with autism spectrum disorder (ASD have comorbid intellectual disability, individuals with higher-functioning autism may not have impaired intellectual functioning but continue to experience deficits in social communication, especially social pragmatics. By contrast, many individuals with an intellectual disability can be very socially engaging (i.e., those with Williams syndrome) but encounter social challenges due to their level of immaturity or naiveté. Because of the difficulties inherent in conducting assessments of those with ASD, the *DSM–5* cautions that IQ scores for this population may be lowered due to problems with social communication and/or behavioral issues rather than intellectual deficits (APA, 2014, p. 40).

Reactive Attachment Disorder

Reactive attachment disorder (RAD) is listed as a disorder with childhood onset by the *DSM-5* in the chapter devoted to "Trauma- and Stressor-Related Disorders". All disorders in this section result from exposure to a traumatic or stressful event. Within this category, there are two disorders that result from neglectful or absent caregiving, and two very different response patterns may result from "social neglect" or "extreme deprivation." On one hand, children may respond with symptoms of emotional withdrawal and inhibition, rarely seeking comfort when distressed, which is the case in reactive attachment disorder (RAD). On the other hand, children may respond with symptoms of inappropriately seeking contact from unfamiliar adults, with no sense of impropriety or social boundaries, leaving themselves vulnerable to strangers. The latter symptoms are characteristic of disinhibited social engagement disorder (DSED). Given the degree of neglect in the formative years, children with reactive attachment disorder often exhibit developmental delays. Differential diagnosis can be made on the basis that although children with an intellectual disability often exhibit social skills commensurate with their intellectual functioning, they do not demonstrate the flat affect or emotion regulation problems seen in those with RAD.

Developmental Delay and Lack of Early Stimulation

By 2 years of age, a child's brain triples in weight (70% of its adult weight). and by 6 years of age, the brain will be 90% of its adult weight (Thatcher, Lyon, Rumsey, & Krasnegor, 1996). Initially the brain is actively involved in creating new neural networks and pruning pathways that are no longer useful or stimulated. Until middle adolescence, periods of prolific creation of connections are followed by periods of pruning. During this period, connections that are frequently used will be strengthened while the least-used connections will be eliminated. Since the formation of neural pathways is dependent on the variety of experiences that a toddler is exposed to, early intervention programs are essential in increasing opportunities for later success. Also, during the first 2 years, glial cells regulate the production and maintenance of myelin, a fatty sheath that coats the nerve fibers creating more efficient message transmission. As a result, preschoolers rapidly improve their skills in such areas as coordination, perception, attention, memory, and language. This was highlighted in our previous discussions of the IDEA 2004 emphasis on early detection of developmental delays and the importance of addressing these delays in the early years (birth to 2 years and 3 to 5 years periods) through the development of intervention plans (IEPs and IFSPs).

Can a quality preschool program enrich learning for those in at-risk situations where stimulation may be minimal and developmental delays may be more pronounced? The Perry Preschool High Scope Program was launched between 1962 and 1967. This longitudinal study investigated whether a high-quality, active learning preschool programs could make a difference for children living in poverty who were at high risk of failing in school. The study has followed the lives of

123 children from African American families who lived in the neighborhood of Perry Elementary School in Ypsilanti, Michigan. Three- and four-year-old children were randomly divided into a program group that received a high-quality preschool program and a comparison group who received no preschool program. The study interviewed the children at various stages of development, and additional information was gathered from the subjects' school, social services, and arrest records. The study found that at age 40, those who enrolled in the preschool program had higher earnings, were more likely to be employed, had significantly fewer arrests, and were more likely to have graduated from college than those who did not (Schweinhart et al., 2005; Schweinhart & Fulcher-Dawson, 2009).

SPECIFIC LEARNING DISABILITIES

Children who exhibit specific learning disabilities (SLD) or specific learning disorders demonstrate specific deficits in academic skill areas (reading, written expression, mathematics), in spite of adequate intellectual functioning (IQ greater than 70 ± 5). These specific deficits are the result of processing problems often related to problems with cognitive fluency, executive processes, or issues with long-term or working memory. These deficits are in contrast to those with an intellectual disability whose low academic skill levels are commensurate with lower scores for general intellectual functioning (IQ less than 70 ± 5). According to the *DSM–5* (APA, 2013), it is possible to diagnose an individual with an intellectual disability as also having a specific learning disability, but only if the difficulties "are in excess of those usually associated with the intellectual disability" (p. 73).

🐟 TEST YOURSELF 🐟

1. The *DSM–5* suggests a cutoff score of 70 ± 5 for an intellectual disability to account for:
   (a) human factors errors.
   (b) potential errors in test administration.
   (c) measurement error.
   (d) variations between different IQ tests.

2. Billy is 24 years old. He had an IQ score of 120, but after a recent car accident where he was thrown out of the window of his car and landed on his head, his IQ is now 70. Would he meet the criteria for an intellectual disability according to the *DSM*?
   (a) No, because his IQ needs to be *below* an IQ of 70.
   (b) No, because we do not know if he has any deficits in adaptive functioning.

(c) Yes, if he also has deficits in the adaptive areas, because his IQ falls within the accepted range.

(d) No, because onset of his reduced brain functioning was not during the developmental period.

3. **Which of the following assumptions is not one of the five assumptions inherent in the definition of an intellectual disability, according to AAIDD?**

(a) Limitations in present functioning must be considered within the context of community environment typical of the individual's age peers and culture.

(b) An important purpose of describing limitations is to develop a profile indicating the severity of the intellectual limitations.

(c) Within an individual, limitations often coexist with strengths.

(d) Valid assessment considers cultural and linguistic diversity as well as differences in communication, sensory, motor, and behavioral factors.

4. **In a study by Wehmeyer and colleagues (2012) on the potential use of technology in supporting individuals with an intellectual disability, the researchers found that individuals with _____ had the highest intensity of support needs.**

(a) a mild intellectual disability

(b) an intellectual disability and physical impairments

(c) an intellectual disability and autism

(d) an intellectual disability and psychiatric disorders

5. **IDEA uses the term "developmental delays" to refer to children who demonstrate all of the following delays except:**

(a) 50% or more delay in one of the developmental areas.

(b) 25% or more delay in two or more of the developmental areas.

(c) delays in social or emotional development.

(d) delays in physical development (motor skills).

6. **Which of the following statements is true? According to IDEA 2004, children over three years of age with identified delays in one of the five developmental areas:**

(a) must be granted access to special education and related services.

(b) may be granted access to special education and related services at the discretion of the state.

(c) must be granted access to special education and related services, but only if the delay causes interference with learning.

(d) must be granted access to special education and related services, but only if the children are between the ages of 3 and 9.

7. **According to the *DSM–IV–TR* APA, 2000), approximately what percentage of children with autism would also have comorbid intellectual disability?**

(a) 50%

(b) 20%

(c) 75%

(d) 60%

8. **It is possible to distinguish between children with reactive attachment disorder (RAD) and an intellectual disability because those with RAD**

(a) are less inhibited socially.

(b) are less responsive to being comforted and are more withdrawn.

(c) have fewer problems with emotion regulation.

(d) are less likely to have been socially neglected.

Answers: 1. c; 2. d; 3. b; 4. b; 5. a; 6. b; 7. c; 8. b

Four

LEGAL ISSUES AND CONCERNS

number of legal issues and concerns have been raised regarding how to best define and conceptualize an intellectual disability (ID) when considering legal questions. These include questions regarding "property ownership, validity of contracts, guardianship, civil or criminal responsibility for a person's actions, educational opportunities, competence to stand trial or participate in legal proceedings, protection from discrimination, and the provision of services, whether these are voluntary or involuntary" (Ellis, 2013, p. 102). We begin this chapter with a developmental and historical focus, initially looking at legal issues in education, the juvenile justice system, and finally legal issues facing adults with an intellectual disability in cases involving criminal or civil law. The chapter will look at how public law reform has shaped the course of service delivery for children with an intellectual disability (IDEA 2004) as well as variations in IQ ranges and terminologies that have been and are currently used to determine cutoff scores in different states for determining eligibility for services for children and adolescents with an intellectual disability.

EDUCATION AND THE LAW: ISSUES AND CONCERNS

In their article "Witnessing Brown," Smith and Kozleski (2005) make a very good argument for the similarities and parallels between individuals with disabilities and individuals who faced racial discrimination based on theories of marginalization. They emphasize that "in most racially desegregated schools, many students continue to be marginalized in subtle and not so subtle ways. The results of this grand experiment suggest that proximity alone does not eliminate the socially constructed boundaries that marginalize some students and privilege others" (p. 271). In 1954, in the case of *Brown v. Board of Education*, the Supreme Court invalidated state laws that sanctioned racial segregation in public

> ## DON'T FORGET
>
> ....
>
> "Marginalization" refers to the concept of the "ingroup" and the "outgroup," where those who are seen as different from the ingroup are marginalized to the position of being outsiders.

primary and secondary schools. Smith and Kozleski (2005) argued that "the narrative for the right-to-education litigation for individuals with disabilities follows the path of Brown." (p. 273).

In 1950, the National Association for Retarded Citizens (NARC) was founded to champion the rights of children with an intellectual disability, since many children with moderate levels of intellectual disability (children with IQs below 50) were excluded from attending public schools, similar to their African American peers. In 1971, the Pennsylvania Association for Retarded Children (PARC) won a right-to-education class action lawsuit, *PARC v. The Commonwealth of Pennsylvania* (1971), citing the case of *Brown v. the Board of Education* and successfully arguing that "the provisions of Pennsylvania state law allowing schools to exclude children with mental retardation from schooling with their peers violated the principles of *Brown v. the Board of Education* decision" (Smith & Kozleski, 2005, p. 273). This ruling won widespread attention and was instrumental in influencing the passage of the Education for All Handicapped Children Act of 1975 (currently known as IDEA 2004), which ensured that all children with disabilities would have access to a free appropriate public education (FAPE) in the least restrictive environment (LRE). When the United States Congress first passed the Education for the Handicapped Act in 1975, the act guaranteed appropriate education of all children with an intellectual disability and developmental disabilities, from school age through 21 years of age (previously discussed in Chapter 3). Amendments to this law now guarantee the right to early intervention for all children with developmental delays or at risk for developmental delays for infants and toddlers until the end of their second year. The way in which an intellectual disability has been conceptualized and the defining criteria have changed over time, depending on the professional source and the prevailing emphasis on genetic or constitutional etiology or function-based definitions. While the medical and psychosocial communities were developing an acceptable definition and classification system for an intellectual disability, the educational community was developing its own system of classification.

Initially the educational classification system was organized around three levels, separating children into three groups based on their predicted ability to learn (Kirk et al., 1955). Children who were deemed *educable* were considered to be capable of learning simple academic skills up to a fourth-grade level. Children were identified as *trainable* if they could be taught how to care for their daily needs but could attain very few academic skills. Finally, the most severe group of children were considered to be *untrainable* or totally dependent and were considered to be in need of long-term care, likely in a residential setting. These terms were refined and adopted by various districts, with the most popular terms being "educable mentally retarded" (EMR) or "educable mentally handicapped" (EMH), used to refer to individuals with an IQ in the range of 55 to 80, or the terms "trainable mentally retarded" (TRM) or "trainable mentally handicapped" (TMH), used to identify individuals with an IQ range of 25 to 50. Today, children who meet criteria for the exceptionality of an intellectual disability are provided with an individualized education program (IEP) that prescribes the nature and extent of available assistance, once they meet the overall criteria for receiving special education and related services for an intellectual disability.

> **DON'T FORGET**
> ....
> According to IDEA 2004, children meet criteria for an intellectual disability if they demonstrate significant difficulties in intellectual and adaptive functioning relative to their peers and the disability interferes with their ability to learn.

Special Education Labels and Placement Decisions

Although the federal guidelines provide the framework for identification of the 13 exceptionalities found in IDEA 2004, it is up to individual school districts to interpret how these regulations apply. Although IDEA provides the funds for special services, how these funds are allocated depends on how the state determines cutoff scores for eligibility to the programs. As a result, there can continue to be variability in the actual IQ scores used for placement purposes. For example, the majority of states suggest a cutoff between 70 and 75 for an intellectual disability program, but some states, such as Iowa, have retained earlier cutoff levels, such as an IQ of 85 (MacMillan & Forness, 1998).

Researchers have investigated classification and placement procedures, and results suggest considerable disparity in how the procedures are defined and applied. MacMillan and Forness (1998) found that there are several reasons why placement decisions may differ, including decisions that are made based on compliance issues (regulations requiring quotas for certain categories or limit the percentage of ethnic population that can be placed in a given category) rather than

DON'T FORGET

Individuals with an intellectual disability demonstrate global or generalized problems in intellectual ability/functioning that influences their learning and adaptive behaviors, while those with specific learning disabilities (SLD) do not have deficits in overall intellectual or cognitive functioning but instead experience deficits in specific skill areas.

predetermined criteria. In one of their investigations, based on data from samples collected in California, MacMillan and Forness (1998), found that less than 14% (6 out of 43) of children who met criteria for an intellectual disability (scoring below an IQ of 75) actually were placed in a program for children with an intellectual disability; instead, 50% of this group were placed in programs for students with specific learning disabilities.

Variations in Definitions of an Intellectual Disability across the United States. As we have already mentioned, IDEA 2004 defines an intellectual disability as one of the 13 exceptionalities having "significantly subaverage general intellectual functioning, existing concurrently with deficits in adaptive behavior and manifested during the developmental period, that adversely affects a child's educational performance" (National Archives and Records Administration, 2005, p. 35836). Although the federal definition provides guidelines for determining eligibility for special education services, states are responsible for adapting these guidelines and proving specific parameters around issues of eligibility. While many organizations recognize the need to consider measurement error when discussing IQ scores (e.g., IQ 70 ± 5), the federal regulations do not address whether or how to account for measurement error. Furthermore, "deficits in adaptive behavior" are even less well defined. Given this latitude, it is not surprising that there are disparities in eligibility criteria with respect to the terms used, cutoff scores applied, and measures of adaptive behavior (Denning, Chamberlain, & Polloway, 2000).

Bergeron, Floyd, and Shands (2008) conducted a study to determine eligibility requirements for an intellectual disability in 50 states and the District of Columbia. They found that the majority of states (53%) used the term "mental retardation," with the terms "mental disability" (12%) and "intellectual disability"(6%) being the other two most commonly used terms. With respect to subclassifying the disability in terms of severity, 18 of the 51 states differentiated severity levels based on IQ. While the most common terms were those used by the *DSM* (mild, moderate, severe, and profound), three states were still using terms (educable MR, trainable MR, and severe/profound MR) that had originated in the 1950s (Kirk et al., 1955).

Examination of actual cutoff scores revealed that the majority (59%) of states used an IQ cutoff of 2 standard deviations (*SD*s) below the mean, which would be the equivalent of an IQ of 70 or below. However, 6% of states used an IQ that fell below 2 *SD*s, which would require an IQ score to be below 70. They found at least one state that required a cutoff score of 78, which would be 1.5 *SD*s below the mean. Surprisingly, many of the states (22%) provided no cutoff scores at all, instead citing the federal guideline "significantly subaverage." The state of Iowa used a noncategorical approach and did not have eligibility criteria specific to an intellectual disability. Two states provided additional criteria to account for exceptions to the rule. In Nebraska, eligibility for services for an intellectual disability depended on meeting one of two potential criteria:

1. An IQ 2 *SD*s below the norm (IQ of 70) with accompanying deficits in adaptive functioning or
2. An IQ of 80 with significant deficits in one or more adaptive skills.

In Wisconsin, although initial eligibility criteria requires an IQ of 70, eligibility criteria change for re-evaluations. In that case, the individual will continue to qualify for services as long as they obtain an IQ between 1 and 2 *SD*s below the norm and the disability is considered to be indefinite.

Bergeron et al. (2008) found considerable variations in how adaptive behaviors were defined and/or suggested ways of measuring them. They found that the vast majority of states (77%) do not provide any cutoff score criteria for determining deficits in adaptive functioning.

DON'T FORGET

Although the federal guidelines do not address the use of the standard error of measure (*SEM*) when making eligibility decisions, Bergeron and colleagues (2008) found that 39% of the state guidelines did specify the use of either a range (IQ 70–75) or refer to the *SEM* when discussing IQ cutoff scores.

Minority Students, Special Education Placement, and an Intellectual Disability. Smith and Kozleski (2005) noted that the "parallel between the National Association for the Advancement of Colored People (NAACP), a civil rights organization for ethnic minorities in the United States, and the Association for Retarded Citizens (ARC) is remarkable," yet they note that "their struggles for equity and access have remained largely separate" (p. 273). It is not difficult to understand how the authors would see the parallels between these two right-to-education groups. However, they also noted that the similarities continue to exist because of special education placements which have seen many minority children join the ranks of children with disabilities, as both are now "resegregated" into special education programs (p. 273).

In their paper regarding achieving equity in special education, Skiba and colleagues (2008) also noted the historical links between special education and the civil rights movement. The California courts found that the use of standardized IQ tests on African American children was unconstitutional for the purposes of placement in programs for the educable mentally retarded (EMR), unless the court provided prior approval for testing (*Larry P. v. Riles*, 1972). However, despite this strong statement, Skiba and colleagues state that the "disproportionate representation of minority students" in special education has continued to exist (Skiba et al., 2008, p. 264). This is not a new revelation. The authors note that Mercer (as cited in Skiba et al., 2008) had documented ethnic differences in rates of special education services as far back as the early 1960s. In her report, Mercer discussed the large numbers of children whom she referred to as "6-hour" or "situationally retarded" children that were identified by the public school systems that tended to identify more children as mentally retarded than any other service providers.

DON'T FORGET

The move to include adaptive behaviors in the definition and identification of those with an intellectual disability was influenced by the fact that some individuals were unable to perform academically but were quite capable of independent living outside of an educational facility.

The concern with disproportionately more minorities in special education was addressed by both the reauthorization of IDEA in 1997 and the latest version, IDEA 2004, that mandates states to monitor disproportionate numbers of children identified and/or placed in special programs. There are several potential ways of monitoring numbers and measuring disproportionality, including: (1) over- or underrepresentation of a given group in a given category, compared to the population at large, or (2) comparing eligibility rates between groups.

Given the IQ cutoff of 70 (±5), it would be estimated that 2% of the population might meet criteria for an intellectual disability based on the IQ criteria. However, when one looks at the number of African American students that are identified as having an intellectual disability, while African American children represent 33% of all those identified, they represent only 17% of the school-aged population. Looking at it from a different angle, using an odds ratio (probability data), African American children are more than twice as likely to be identified as having an intellectual disability than White students (Skiba et al., 2008). Parrish (2002) reported that in at least 45 states, African American children in special education are extensively overrepresented in some categories and that they are at the highest risk for being identified with an intellectual disability.

Several hypotheses have been put forward to account for the disproportion in identification and placement, including the possibility of test bias and the influence of poverty and inequality of school opportunities. However, research results have been inconclusive in demonstrating any single or combined sources for the disparity in identification and placement of African American students with an intellectual disability in the education system.

The Legal System: Issues and Concerns

According to Ellis (2013), the term " intellectual disability" can be described differently by different professions, with more medically or mental health–related professions seeing an intellectual disability as a mental disorder, such as in "mental illness," the legal profession finds it most useful to consider an intellectual disability as a physical disability (more similar to a physical impairment, like deafness or blindness) rather than a disorder, since "the law's concern in dealing with a person with an intellectual disability is almost always with that person's functional abilities and limitations in society. This concern is reflected in various aspects of criminal and civil law, although the methods of assessing those functional abilities and limitations have changed considerably over time" (p. 107).

In this section, we discuss how an intellectual disability is conceptualized in civil and criminal law, beginning with the juvenile justice system.

Juvenile Justice System: Issues and Concerns. Chapter 2 discussed several subtypes of intellectual disabilities, including fetal alcohol syndrome (FAS) and fetal alcohol spectrum disorder (FASD). Although individuals who have the more severe forms of FAS often can be physically recognized by characteristics such as facial anomalies, those with the more subtle forms of the disorder (FASD) often are undetected and undiagnosed (Little, Snell, Rosenfeld, Gilstrap, & Gant, 1990). Studies have shown that there is an increased risk for adolescents with FASD to become involved in the juvenile justice system (Streissguth et al., 2004b), due to problems in areas of an intellectual disability, hyperactivity/impulsivity, and poor social skills (Substance Abuse and Mental Health Services Administration [SAMHSA], 2007). According to SAMSHA (2007), youth with FASD who are impulsive do not consider the consequences of their actions, and their poor sense of personal boundaries makes them vulnerable to peer pressure and gang-related activities. These youth pose a challenge to the juvenile justice system because they also often do not have the ability to understand legal proceedings. Because of their vulnerability and lack of understanding, SAMHSA made several recommendations to prepare advocates to assist youth entering the juvenile justice system, including screening for FASD at all entry points into the judicial system. SAMHSA urges attorneys to become familiar with FASD and the consequences this can have on the ability of youth with FAS/FASD to:

- comprehend the charges and participate in their own defense.
- distinguish right from wrong (diminished capacity).
- make decisions to decline/remand/waive their rights (juvenile rather than adult facility).
- understand sentencing.
- profit from treatment (appropriate court-ordered interventions).

The SAMHSA (2007) report also emphasizes that incarceration can increase the risk of reoffending through deviancy training (vulnerability to be influenced by other youth in detention). It recommends instead that probation or aftercare be an alternative to incarceration to provide a supervised and structured situation where skills can be monitored.

Civil and Criminal Law: Issues and Concerns. In courts of law, individuals with an intellectual disability have been identified for differential treatment based on the functional consequences of their condition (mental capacity or diminished capacity) rather than on the basis of its classification as a mental disorder or its etiology. For example, in the criminal justice system, there are two important decisions that must be made:

1. A defendant's responsibility for committing a crime (knowing wrong from right/ability to control impulses).
2. His or her capacity to contribute toward a defense (capacity to stand trial) (Comer, 2010).

These two fundamental questions focus on an individual's competence to stand trial and competence to contribute to his or her own defense. This is similar to what is required when an individual stands trial for a crime and opts for an insanity plea. In that case, the courts must determine if the individual was competent at the time of committing the crime (right from wrong) and furthermore are they competent at this time to stand trial (contribute to his or her own trial). If they are not competent to stand trial, then he or she is housed in a mental health facility until competent to stand trial.

If there is a question as to whether a particular defendant is competent to stand trial, the legal test will be whether, because of his or her mental condition, "he [or she] has sufficient present ability to consult with his [or her] lawyer with a reasonable degree of rational understanding—and whether he [or she] has a rational as well as factual understanding of the proceedings against him [or her]" (Ellis, 2013, p. 103). The same focus on the potential impairment in an individual's functioning guides civil court proceedings; for example, issues of guardianship and an individual's ability or inability to manage their own affairs (personal or financial). According to Ellis (2013), in a court of law, it does not matter why an individual has impaired functioning (e.g., an intellectual disability versus mental illness versus dementia) since the focus is on the outcome (degree of challenges and limitations that impaired functioning causes) so that appropriate accommodations can be made.

DON'T FORGET

In the United States, there are two different criminal law procedures for determining an insanity plea: the *McNaghten* Test (1843), which is currently used in 26 states, and the *American Law Institute* (1955) ruling, currently used in 22 states. Three states (Montana, Idaho, and Utah) do not have an insanity plea. The McNaghten Test asks whether the individual knew right from wrong, while the American Law Institute requires that an individual has a disorder that (a) prevents him or her knowing right from wrong and (b) prevents him or her from controlling impulses (Comer, 2010).

Olley (2013) provides a different perspective than Ellis (2013) regarding defining an intellectual disability, especially in the case of criminal court investigations. Citing the *Atkins v. Virginia* US Supreme Court decision (2002), which prohibits the use of the death penalty for individuals with an intellectual disability, Olley pointed out that it was important that wording in definitions be very clear and objective since this may have life-or-death consequences. Olley argued that although "competence to stand trial" is not limited to those with an intellectual disability, it is very important to determine whether individuals with an intellectual disability can meet this standard, often referred to as the *Dusky* standard; this was based on the ruling of *Dusky v. United States* (1960), when the US Supreme Court ruled that "defendants cannot be brought to trial unless they understand the charges against them and are able to assist their attorney in their own defense" Olley (2013, p. 118).

In the case of *Atkins v. Virginia*, the Supreme Court recognized that individuals with an intellectual disability have diminished capacities to understand and process information, to communicate, to generalize from previous mistakes and profit from new experiences, to engage in logical reasoning, to control impulses, to correctly read the nuances of social situations and intentions of others, and to understand the reactions of others. Given these characteristics, it is not surprising to find that individuals with an intellectual disability who are charged with serious crimes are vulnerable to the justice system's common proceedings, rules, and regulations. Everington and Keyes (1999, p. 31) summarized these vulnerabilities in the following way:

> Certain characteristics are more common to members of this population, including: poor memory (does not attend to details and poor recall), significantly reduced intelligence, poor ability to use abstract thought (very rigid and concrete in their thought patterns), problems with concentration or focusing (easily distractible), poor transference and generalization skills (unable to make logical connections), impulsive behaviors (difficulty controlling repetitive and inappropriate behaviors, poor planning and coping skills (unable to see cause/effect; easily frustrated), poor judgment skills (unable to recognize dangerous situations), and a tendency to acquiesce (in order to please significant others and those in authority).

Given these traits, it is not surprising that individuals with an intellectual disability become vulnerable to systems that can be highly intimidating. Nowhere is this more prevalent than in the case of eliciting false confessions from individuals with an intellectual disability. According to Kassin (2005), there are two populations that are at high risk for false confessions: younger defendants and individuals with an intellectual disability. Kassin suggests a range of influences that are behind false confessions, including misguided attempts to protect or help the real assailant, fears of retaliation, or an exhausted plea to end a process that has been intellectually and emotionally overwhelming. In one study, Leo and Ofshe (1998) found that an overwhelming majority of cases (8 out of 9) that had been overturned involved a false confession from a person with an intellectual disability. Close and Walker (2010) suggested that individuals with an intellectual disability are often not provided with opportunities to respond to the challenges they face in the criminal justice system in a way that would assist them in coping with the complexities of the system. In their article about the challenges that individuals with an intellectual disability face in the judicial system, Close and Walker suggest that the time has come for forensic special educators (FSE) to serve in the capacity of experts who are knowledgeable about both the judicial system and the characteristics of persons with developmental disabilities. They argue that the FSE knowledge of functional behavioral analysis and an intellectual disability would provide the background for preparing individuals for court appearances and educating attorneys about the salient characteristics that might influence judicial decisions negatively.

According to Olley (2013), although the *Dusky* standard is interpreted differently by different states, it would certainly assist individuals who do competence evaluations and their attorneys, if there were a clear objective definition for an intellectual disability. Olley criticized the contemporary definition provided by AAIDD (AAIDD, 2010) as a less rigid definition of an intellectual disability that downplays the use of IQ scores and has implied that limitations in adaptive functioning are caused by limitations in IQ, which further complicates an already strained relationship between these two criteria. Furthermore, Olley states that the majority of states that have the death penalty require that an individual be deemed impaired in both intellectual and adaptive functioning. Although it is possible to conduct an assessment of intelligence in a prison, he reminded the reader that "AAIDD ... [has] emphasized that adaptive functioning is typical community functioning which cannot be validly assessed in jail or prison" (AAIDD, 2010, p. 120). Clearly, according to Olley (2013), changes in the current definition of an intellectual disability could have dire consequences for individuals with an intellectual disability charged with criminal offenses.

Civil Rights Laws. The Americans with Disabilities Act Amendments Act of 2008 (ADAAA) and Section 504 of the Rehabilitation Act of 1973 are civil rights laws protecting the rights of individuals with disabilities. ADAAA was passed by Congress in December 2008 and is an update of the previous civil rights law, the Americans with Disabilities Act (ADA) of 1990.

ADAAA prohibits discrimination on the basis of disability in employment, public services, and accommodations needed to perform major life activities, such as: caring for oneself, performing manual tasks, seeing, hearing, speaking, breathing, learning, and working. In addition to these basic life tasks, the new version (ADAAA, 2008) added several other life activities that may also require accommodations in order for individuals with disabilities to perform essential job functions: eating, sleeping, walking, standing lifting, bending, reading, concentrating, thinking, and communicating. Examples of reasonable accommodations include: installing ramps, removing transportation barriers, and providing alternate communication forms (e.g., telecommunication systems, etc.). ADAAA also protects students who may have community job placements, if these placements require disability accommodations.

The statute defines "mental disabilities" as "any mental or psychological disorder, such as mental retardation, organic brain syndrome, emotional or mental illness, and specific learning disabilities" (Parry, 1997, p. 9). However, although the statute refers to the term "disorder," the scope of the law's actual protection extends only to disabilities that substantially limit major life activities (working, learning, self-care, interacting with others, etc.), and whether a particular individual's impairment is "substantial" is the issue, which has caused significant concern for many individuals who seek accommodations under ADAAA.

Section 504 is a federal law that also protects the rights of individuals with disabilities who are enrolled in programs and activities that are federally funded and receive financial assistance from the US Department of Education. Under Section 504, school districts are mandated to provide a free "appropriate" public education and provide the necessary accommodations regardless of the nature or severity of the disability, as long as the disability interferes with a major life activity.

It is important to know that both ADAAA and Section 504 provide only a vague description of what constitutes a "disability," which is recognized as:

1. a physical or mental impairment that significantly limits one or more major life activities;
2. a record of such impairment; or
3. is recognized as having an impairment.

Ellis (1992) points out that as our understanding of disabilities and the rights of individuals with disabilities increases, decisions sometimes require "a delicate balance" between protecting the individuals from harm, on the one hand, and enhancing their independence and autonomy in their lives.

DON'T FORGET

Any student who qualifies for special education services under IDEA 2004 would also be eligible under Section 504, but the reverse is not necessarily true (students receiving support under Section 504 may not be eligible for services under IDEA).

TEST YOURSELF

1. In the case of *Brown v. Board of Education*, the Supreme Court ruled that:
   (a) individuals could not be segregated from public schools on the basis of color.
   (b) individuals could not be segregated from public elementary and secondary schools on the basis of color.
   (c) children of color could not be denied special education services.
   (d) assessments of children's intelligence needed to have prior approval by the courts.

2. **Educationally, terms used to differentiate children on the basis of their intellectual abilities initially included:**
   (a) mild, severe, profound.
   (b) mild, moderate, and severe/profound.
   (c) educable, trainable, and untrainable.
   (d) Tier I, Tier II, and Tier III services.

3. **In their study of the use of different terms across the United States, Bergeron et al. (2008) found that the most common term used to identify individuals with low intellectual functioning was:**
   (a) mentally deficient.
   (b) intellectual disability.
   (c) mental disability.
   (d) mental retardation.

4. **In the same study by Bergeron et al. (2008), the authors found that _____ % of states provided no IQ cutoff scores in their eligibility requirements for an intellectual disability:**
   (a) 10%
   (b) 22%
   (c) 5%
   (d) 43%

5. **In the articles by Smith and Kozleski (2005) and Skiba and colleagues (2008), the researchers noted the similarities between:**
   (a) individuals with a specific learning disability and an intellectual disability.
   (b) youth with an intellectual disability and autism spectrum disorder.
   (c) the historical links between special education and the civil rights movement.
   (d) disparities in protections offered by ADA/ADAAA.

6. **Skiba and colleagues (2008) found that although African American children represent 17% of the population of school-aged children, they represented _____ of the special education recipients identified as having an intellectual disability.**
   (a) 25%
   (b) 50%
   (c) 17%
   (d) 33%

7. **In the case of *Atkins v. Virginia*, the decision handed down by the Supreme Court was that:**
   (a) individuals have a duty to report suspected child abuse.
   (b) the death penalty is prohibited for those with an intellectual disability.
   (c) the courts have to prove that an individual is competent to stand trial.
   (d) the burden of proof is on the plaintiff in cases where the defendant has an intellectual disability.

8. **According to Kassin (2005), the two populations that are at highest risk for false confessions are:**
   (a) young offenders and individuals with an intellectual disability.
   (b) individuals with emotional disorders and an intellectual disability.
   (c) individuals with an intellectual disability and autism spectrum disorder.
   (d) females.

Answers: 1. b; 2. c; 3. d; 4. b; 5. c; 6. d; 7. b; 8. a

Five

THEORIES OF INTELLIGENCE AND THE FLYNN EFFECT

I t is important that a practitioner administering intelligence tests be familiar with the theories behind those tests. Theories of the structure of intellectual abilities help to guide the development of these measures and, consequently, can direct the practitioner's interpretation of an examinee's scores. This chapter provides an overview of some of the major theories behind intelligence tests. For more detailed information about the theories of specific intelligence measures, refer to other books in this *Essentials* series.

SPEARMAN'S TWO-FACTOR THEORY

Charles Spearman (1904) developed a two-factor theory of intelligence early in the 20th century. Using factor analysis, he tested his hypothesis that there was single dimension accounted for the correlations among all mental ability tests. Spearman termed this dimension "general intelligence," or "g." He determined that this single g factor was correlated with specific abilities (s). He believed that these two factors accounted for the mathematical variance in each of the measured variables, although he regarded g as the most important factor (Schlinger, 2003). Individual differences in g "reflect individual differences in mental energy, and individual differences in mental energy lead to individual differences in performance on all ability tests and therefore account for the correlations among all tests of mental ability" (Reschly, Myers, & Hartel, 2002, p. 77).

DON'T FORGET
....
The idea of g is used to represent the term "general intelligence." More than a century after this term was developed, we still use it.

THURSTONE'S PRIMARY MENTAL ABILITIES

Louis Leon Thurstone conducted research in the 1930s to identify the dimensions of ability (intelligence). He and his colleagues observed seven factors across many different analyses that they called "primary mental abilities" (Thurstone, 1938). According to Reschly et al. (2002), "the correlations among the primary mental abilities were well described by a single second-order factor, which Thurstone and Thurstone argued provided a way to reconcile Spearman's theory with their own. That is, at the level of the primary mental abilities, seven dimensions were required to represent the relations among a large set of tests" (p. 79).

These seven primary mental abilities are: (1) verbal comprehension, (2) word fluency, (3) spatial ability, (4) memory, (5) numerical facility, (6) perceptual speed, and (7) reasoning. Thurstone (1938) said that the primary mental abilities were trivial and too narrow. He believed that *g*, the second-order general factor, should be considered the primary factor.

DON'T FORGET

Brain mapping was in its infancy in the 1930s, but Thurstone believed that the future would bring a mapping of mental abilities onto brain areas. He thought that each ability factor eventually would be found to relate to a particular area of the brain area.

CATTELL-HORN-CARROLL THEORY

The Cattell-Horn-Carroll (CHC) theory is based on the work of Raymond Cattell, John Horn, and John Carroll. CHC began with the *Gf-Gc* (fluid and crystallized intelligence, respectively) theory of Cattell and Horn (Horn & Cattell, 1966); Carroll added his three-stratum theory. These two theories had a similar approach to the structure of human cognitive abilities and complemented one another reasonably well. Work by McGrew and Flanagan (1998), updated later by Flanagan, McGrew, and Ortiz (2000), added to the theoretical approach. CHC integrates the concept of a general intelligence with the concept of several different aspects of intelligence.

The original CHC theory views intelligence as being comprised of 9 broad abilities and more than 70 narrow abilities. With the recent revisions to the theory, the theoretical approach now includes 16 broad cognitive abilities and more than 80 narrow abilities. For brevity, we focus on the 16 broad cognitive abilities. Their relationship to current intelligence measures will be clear.

Fluid Intelligence The mental operations that someone uses to solve a novel task that cannot be performed automatically. Examples include drawing inferences, extrapolating information, problem solving, and forming and recognizing concepts.

Crystallized Intelligence The depth and breadth of someone's acquired knowledge. It includes both declarative and procedural knowledge. Declarative knowledge involves things such as facts, concepts, and rules; this information is held in someone's long-term memory and is activated when there is related information in their working memory. Procedural knowledge involves the process of reasoning with previously learned procedures in an effort to transform knowledge.

General (Domain-Specific) Knowledge The depth and breadth of someone's specialized knowledge. Since it is specialized, it can develop through someone's work experience, interests, or hobbies.

Quantitative Knowledge The depth and breadth of someone's mathematical knowledge.

Reading/Writing Ability The knowledge acquired to solve both basic and complex problems in the areas of basic reading, reading fluency, and written expression.

Short-Term Memory The ability to collect and hold information and then use it within several seconds.

Long-Term Storage and Retrieval The ability to store information and retrieve new or previously acquired information from long-term memory.

Visual Processing The ability to generate, store, retrieve, analyze, synthesize, and think with visual patterns and stimuli.

Auditory Processing The ability to perceive, analyze, and synthesize auditory stimuli patterns and discriminate nuances in sound patterns and speech.

Olfactory Abilities The ability to detect, process, and interpret information from the olfactory system.

Tactile Abilities The ability to detect, process, and interpret information in haptic (touch) sensations.

Psychomotor Abilities The ability to move fingers, hands, and legs with precision, coordination, or strength.

Kinesthetic Abilities The ability to detect and process information in sensations of a person's awareness of body position and movement.

Processing Speed The ability to perform simple and repetitive cognitive tasks fluently and quickly.

Decision Speed/Reaction Time The ability to react quickly and make decisions.

Psychomotor Speed The ability to engage physical body movements quickly and fluidly.

DON'T FORGET

A practitioner who currently uses intelligence tests should think about the CHC theory and how the broad cognitive abilities relate to the test(s) being administered. Consideration should be given to how closely the CHC theory matches their test choice.

TRIARCHIC THEORY OF INTELLIGENCE

Robert Sternberg's (1985) triarchic theory of intelligence is based on three subtheories. These subtheories, which offer a general view of intelligence and address the types of tasks used to measure intelligence, are componential intelligence, experiential intelligence, and practical intelligence.

Componential Intelligence Relates a person's intelligence to his or her internal world. It addresses the mental mechanisms that are associated with different levels of intelligence. Different information processing components are needed to learn how to do things, plan what to do and how to do them, and then do them.

Experiential Intelligence Relates a person's intelligence to a continuum of his or her experiences with tasks or situations. It focuses on both the novelty and automatization of tasks.

Practical Intelligence Relates a person's intelligence to his or her external world. It includes three types of acts that describe everyday intelligent behavior: environmental adaptation, selection, and shaping.

PLANNING, ATTENTION-AROUSAL, SIMULTANEOUS, AND SUCCESSIVE THEORY OF INTELLIGENCE

Based on the work of Alexander Luria (1966) on brain structure, the Planning, Attention-Arousal, Simultaneous, and Successive (PASS) theory of intelligence was proposed initially by J. P. Das, J. R. Kirby, and R. F. Jarman in 1975. It was later revised (see Das, Naglieri & Kirby, 1994; Das, Kar & Parrila, 1996). This theory suggests that our cognition uses three systems (planning, attention and arousal, and simultaneous and successive processing) and four processes for organization.

Planning Process Involves the executive functions that control and organize behavior, select and construct cognitive strategies, and monitor performance.

Attention-Arousal Process Helps to maintain our arousal levels and alertness, thus allowing us to attend to stimuli.

Simultaneous Processing Requires us to integrate separate stimuli into whole units of information.

Successive Processing Involves our ability to integrate stimuli into a sequential order.

DON'T FORGET

An informative book about the PASS theory is *Assessment of Cognitive Processes: The PASS Theory of Intelligence*, by J. P. Das, Jack Naglieri, and John Kirby (1994).

THEORY OF MULTIPLE INTELLIGENCES

Howard Gardner (1983) proposed a theory of multiple intelligences (MI theory) that was quite different from previous theories. Its attractiveness, to some, is the fact that it does not rely on factor analysis. Rather, as Kaufman, Kaufman, and Plucker (2013, p. 813) indicated, it is based on an analysis of the research using eight criteria:

(a) potential isolation by brain damage, (b) the existence of idiot savants, prodigies, and other exceptional individuals, (c) an identifiable core operation or set of operations, (d) a distinctive development history (i.e., it should be possible to differentiate experts from novices in the domain), (e) an evolutionary history and evolutionary plausibility (i.e., its precursors should be evident in less evolved species), (f) support from experimental psychological tasks, (g) support from psychometric findings, and (h) susceptibility to encoding in a symbol system.

Gardner suggested that there are eight intelligences: (1) linguistic, (2) logical-mathematical, (3) spatial, (4) bodily kinesthetic, (5) musical, (6) interpersonal, (7) intrapersonal, and (8) naturalistic. Additional intelligences, such as spiritual and existential intelligences, could be added to the theory (Gardner, 1999). Gardner

DON'T FORGET

Gardner's theory of multiple intelligences is fluid. He and others have contemplated adding other intelligences beyond those that we typically attribute to the theory. Stay tuned!

and Moran (2006) stated that Gardner "maintains that relatively independent yet interacting intelligences provide a better understanding of the variety and scope of human cognitive feats than do competing accounts (p. 227)."

FLYNN EFFECT

The "Flynn effect" is a term that arose from the work of James Flynn (Flynn, 1984; McGrew, 2010). Flynn's work highlighted the fact that the general IQ score of an individual increases over time. Since the creation of intelligence tests, IQ scores have increased with each generation. On average, Flynn noticed that IQ scores rose about 0.30 points each year, or roughly 3 points per decade.

Flynn's work began in the 1980s, but in 2012, he affirmed the phenomenon initially observed. In his book *Are We Getting Smarter?: Rising IQ in the Twenty-First Century*, Flynn indicated that the increase in IQ occurs not only in the United States but around the world. He reports evidence of "IQ gains proceeding at 0.30 points per year over the last half of the twentieth century, a rate often found in other nations, for a total gain of over 15 points" (p. 6).

> ### CAUTION
> ....
> Always use the most recent version of an intelligence test. It will have the most up-to-date norms and can provide with a score that best reflects an examinee's intelligence level.

The Flynn Effect on an Intellectual Disability Diagnosis

Intelligence tests are standardized on the current population. Samples of the general population are used in the standardization process and reflect the performance of those taking the test. The Flynn effect may have implications on the diagnosis of an intellectual disability (ID). The diagnostic criteria for an intellectual disability include a score "of approximately two standard deviations *(SDs)* or more below the population mean, including a margin for measurement error (generally +5 points)" (American Psychiatric Association, 2013, p. 37). For a test with a mean of 100 and an *SD* of 15 points, a score of 70 (or 75 with measurement error) may indicate the presence of an intellectual disability. McGrew (2011) noted that courts should embrace the concept of the standard error of measurement (SEM).

If an examiner is not using the latest version of an intelligence test, the score obtained may be an overestimate of the examinee's intelligence level. Take, for example, the Wechsler Intelligence Scale for Children (WISC), one of the most widely used intelligence tests. Developed in 1949 by David Wechsler, the WISC was revised in 1974 (WISC–R), 1991 (WISC–III), 2003 (WISC–IV), and 2014 (WISC–V). Let's say a person in 2016 was given a WISC–III (with 1991 norms) and his score was 76. If we take into account the 3-point rise in IQ each decade, this same individual might receive an IQ score of 70 if he was administered the WISC–V, published about two decades after the WISC–R. The IQ score of 70 is actually 2 SDs below the mean and may be an indication of a potential intellectual disability. The score of 76 is higher than the score of 70 since the WISC–III has outdated norms. As Flynn (2012) noted: "Unless we adjust IQs for obsolete norms, the death penalty becomes a lottery. You take a test with current norms and your IQ is 70. But if you are unlucky enough to take a test with norms 20 years obsolete, the very same performance will get an IQ of 76 and you will be executed" (p. 67). As Kaufman and Weiss (2010) indicated, "If a convicted criminal in a capital punishment case earned a global IQ of 73 on a test with 20-year old norms, should that IQ be adjusted by 6 points to account for their datedness? Is the best estimate of the person's mental functioning 73 or 67?" (p. 380).

A major question surrounding the Flynn effect is the etiology of the phenomenon. Kaufman and Weiss (2010) reported that researchers differ as to why they believe the Flynn effect occurs. They indicate that research points to genetics (e.g., Rogers & Wanstrom, 2007), education (e.g., Teasdale & Owen, 2005), environmental factors such as nutrition (e.g., Colon, Lluis-Font & Andres-Pueyo, 2005), and/or public health improvements (e.g., Steen, 2009). As Zhou, Zhu, and Weiss (2010) pointed out, "much is still left to be learned about the nature of this phenomenon" (p. 400).

Another question that arises from the discussion of the Flynn effect relates to the structure of intelligence tests. One problem is the assumption that newer tests measure the same thing as the ones they replace; however, according to Sternberg (2010), we "should not immediately assume that the successive editions actually measure quite the same construct" (p. 435). This is a very important factor to consider; if a test revision is qualitatively different from the last edition, then the differences in scores may not be meaningful. Differences may be attributed to a change in content rather than an increase in intelligence. As Sternberg noted, "We should not assume that because the name of a test stays the same, the actual constructs measured stay just the same as well."

The Flynn Effect and High-Stakes Decisions

There also is disagreement as to whether IQ scores should be corrected for the Flynn effect in high-stakes decisions, such as capital punishment cases, which we discuss next. According to Fletcher, Stuebing, and Hughes (2010), these scores should be corrected in cases where a test with older norms was used. As they asked, "Should an offender be executed because the psychologist who gave the WISC failed to write a note indicating that the IQ score may be an overestimate because of norms [*sic*] obsolescence?" (p. 470). Correcting an IQ score is considered an appropriate normative comparison (Gresham, 2009).

DON'T FORGET

Read all about the Flynn effect in James Flynn's book, *Are We Getting Smarter? Rising IQ in the Twenty-First Century* (2012).

Conversely, Hagan, Drogin, and Guilmette (2010) stated IQ scores should *not* be adjusted for the Flynn effect in capital punishment cases. Their review of work by Duvall and Morris (2006) indicate that "None of the 38 states allowing for capital punishment has a statute mandating reduction of a capital defendant's IQ scores based on the [Flynn effect]" (Hagan, Drogin, & Guilmette, 2010, p. 475).

INTELLECTUAL DISABILITY AND CAPITAL PUNISHMENT CASES

There is controversy surrounding capital punishment cases and individuals with disabilities. It has been argued that individuals with low IQs are unable to understand the consequences of their criminal behavior. Sternberg (2010) has suggested that "the very use of IQ in such [criminal] proceedings is ethically challenged, because such tests measure cognitive intelligence, not ethical intelligence" since

DON'T FORGET

The US Supreme Court hears cases that relate to the work of psychologists and school psychologists. To read about new cases, you can search at:
http://www.supremecourt.gov/case_documents.aspx

"ethical intelligence—one's level of ethical reasoning and problem solving—may be more relevant than cognitive intelligence in such cases" (p. 435). Several cases of defendants with low IQs have made it to the US Supreme Court, allowing justices to weigh in on this topic. We address a few cases with which readers should be familiar.

Penry v. Lynaugh (1989)

In 1989, John Paul Penry was charged and ultimately convicted of 1979 rape and murder. The judge in the case ruled that Penry was competent to stand trial, "although a psychologist testified that he was mildly to moderately retarded and had the mental age of a six-year-old" (Palmer, 2008, p. 416). After Penry was sentenced to death, his case went to the Texas Court of Criminal Appeals and reached the Supreme Court. The Court determined there was no national consensus barring individuals with a disability from receiving the death penalty (Blume & Salekin, 2015). The justices ruled that the death sentence in this case did not violate the Eighth Amendment's ban on cruel and unusual punishment.

Atkins v. Virginia (2002)

In the case of *Atkins v. Virginia* (2002), Daryl Atkins stood trial for murder. A psychologist reported that he had an IQ score of 59 and indicated that Atkins was mildly mentally retarded (Shannon, 2003). The case ultimately was heard by the US Supreme Court, where the justices ruled that sentencing people with intellectual disabilities to death violated the ban on cruel and unusual punishment of the Eighth and Fourteenth Amendments. To be considered as having an intellectual disability, a person must have subaverage intellectual functioning and a lack of fundamental social and practical skills; both of these deficits must have been present before the age of 18. If these conditions are met, a person is deemed ineligible for the death penalty. Therefore, the Court forbade the execution of individuals with an intellectual disability. Taylor and Krauss (2014) noted: "The court reasoned that offenders with intellectual disabilities had significant impairments in their abilities to process information, logically reason, control their impulses and learn from experience. These factors made them both less morally culpable and more susceptible to wrongful conviction" (p. 26). Discretion was given to the states about how they would implement the Court's decision.

Hall v. Florida (2014)

A dozen years after *Atkins v. Virginia*, the US Supreme Court ruled again, this time in *Hall v. Florida* (2014). In this case, Freddie Lee Hall was convicted of murder. The Florida Supreme Court in 2012 "ruled that Mr. Hall was eligible to be executed because his I.Q. had been measured at various times as 71, 73 and 80" (Liptak, 2014). The court also prohibited states from using only intelligence test scores in cases where a person presents with an IQ in the 70 to 75 range. Because these tests have a *SEM*, someone with an IQ of 71, such as Hall, actually may have an intellectual disability. Thus, the Court narrowed the discretion states have in determining whether an individual has an intellectual disability and can be executed. Warlick and Dougherty (2015) noted "although the Supreme Court's

May 2014 decision overturned the prior decisions of Florida's courts, it did not rule that Hall was ineligible for execution. It did find that Florida's bright-line IQ cutoff—requiring admissible proof of an IQ score of 70 or below—was unconstitutional" (p. 5).

The American Association on Intellectual and Developmental Disabilities (AAIDD) and The Arc collaborated on a position statement on the criminal justice system and individuals with an intellectual disability and/or developmental disability. You can read the position statement in **Appendix B**.

🖋 TEST YOURSELF 🖋

1. **Recent revisions to the CHC theory of intelligence indicate which cognitive structure?**
   (a) 12 broad and more than 60 narrow abilities
   (b) 16 broad and more than 80 narrow abilities
   (c) 10 broad and more than 50 narrow abilities
   (d) 14 broad and more than 40 narrow abilities

2. **In which US Supreme Court case did the Court rule that the death sentence did not violate the Eighth Amendment's ban on cruel and unusual punishment?**
   (a) *Milner v. New York*
   (b) *Hall v. Florida*
   (c) *Atkins v. Virginia*
   (d) *Penry v. Lynaugh*

3. **What are the three subtheories of the triarchic theory of intelligence?**
   (a) Temperamental, experiential, realistic
   (b) Experimental, componential, practical
   (c) Motivational, therapeutic, experiential
   (d) Componential, experiential, practical

4. **The Flynn effect refers to which change in IQ score?**
   (a) 1 standard deviation increase each 15 years
   (b) 1 standard deviation increase each 20 years
   (c) A 3-point increase each decade
   (d) ±5 points each decade

5. **Which intelligence is being considered as an addition to the theory on multiple intelligences?**
   (a) Quizzical
   (b) Inspirational
   (c) Motivational
   (d) Existential

6. **Which US Supreme Court case(s) prohibit(s) states from using only intelligence test scores in cases where a person presents with an IQ in the 70 to 75 range?**
   (a) *Atkins v. Virginia*
   (b) *Penry v. Lynaugh*
   (c) *Hall v. Florida*
   (d) *Osmark v. California*

7. **The PASS theory of intelligence references which four processes?**
   (a) Planning, Attention-Arousal, Simultaneous, Successive
   (b) Preferential, Academic, Sequential, Standardization
   (c) Psychological, Academic, Successive, Sequential
   (d) Preferential, Assertive, Singular, Simultaneous

8. **In which case did the US Supreme Court rule that sentencing people with intellectual disabilities to death violated the ban on cruel and unusual punishment in the Eighth and Fourteenth Amendments?**
   (a) *Penry v. Lynaugh*
   (b) *Chauncy v. Wilder*
   (c) *Atkins v. Virginia*
   (d) *Hall v. Florida*

Answers: 1. b; 2. d; 3. d; 4. c; 5. d; 6. c; 7. a; 8. C

Six

ASSESSMENT OF AN INTELLECTUAL DISABILITY

The American Association on Intellectual and Developmental Disabilities (AAIDD), which began in 1876, has created guidelines to name, define, and diagnose what we now call an intellectual disability. In 2010, AAIDD revised its definition and diagnostic criteria of an intellectual disability and published the 11th edition of *Intellectual Disability: Definition, Classification, and Systems of Supports* (AAIDD, 2010). The new edition was published in response to the evolution of scientific knowledge and our understanding of the disorder.

In 2002, AAIDD developed a framework for the assessment of an intellectual disability (AAIDD, 2010) (see **Rapid Reference** 6.1). This proposed framework focused on the three functions of diagnosis, classification, and planning supports. Practitioners can use the framework to develop an appropriate battery for the assessment of an intellectual disability. According to AAIDD (2010), "assessment in the field of ID is conducted in order to diagnose a disability, classify by relevant characteristics, and plan for an individual's needed supports" (p. 22). Since the focus of this book is on assessment, we concentrate on designing appropriate test batteries. In this chapter, we address some assessment measures that can be used to assess intelligence, adaptive behavior, development and school readiness, achievement, and behavior. Chapter 7 includes two sample reports.

CAUTION
....
When designing an assessment battery, choose measures that are appropriate for an individual's ability level.

≡ Rapid Reference 6.1 AAIDD's Framework for Assessment

....

Assessment Function	Specific Purpose	Examples of Measures, Tools, and Assessment Methods
Diagnosis	• Establish presence or absence of intellectual disability • Establish eligibility for services • Establish eligibility for benefits • Establish eligibility for legal protections	• Intelligence tests • Adaptive behavior scales • Documented age of onset • Developmental measures • Social history and educational records
Classification	• Classify for intensity of needed support(s) • Classify for research purposes • Classify by selected characteristics • Classify for special education supports • Classify for reimbursement/ funding	• Supports needs intensity scales • Levels of adaptive behavior • IQ ranges or levels • Environmental assessment • Etiology-risk factor systems • Mental health measures • Benefit categories
Planning and developing a systems of supports	• Support to enhance human functioning • Support to improve outcomes • Support to help implement person's choices • Support to assure human rights	• Person-centered planning • Self-appraisal • Ecological inventory • Developmental tests • Speech/language, motor, sensory assessment • Achievement tests • Support needs intensity scales • Functional behavioral assessment • Behavior support plan • Family centered support plan • Individualized Family Support Plan, Individualized Education Program, Individualized Transition Plan • Self-directed plan

Source: AAIDD, 2010, p. 23.

DESIGNING A TEST BATTERY

An assessment battery will include a variety of tests. The choice of tests will depend on the student being tested, his or her ability level, and the tests that are available. Let's first address the student who is being evaluated.

Student

A student may be assessed for an initial evaluation or a reevaluation. In the case of an initial evaluation for an intellectual disability, it is most likely that the child is in elementary school. There are cases where we have done an initial assessment on a student in middle school, but most times, the student was in a private school or was homeschooled during the elementary years.

Students may present with a variety of issues, and it may take a multidisciplinary team to assess all of the areas of deficit. A speech-language pathologist may conduct an assessment to evaluate students' expressive and receptive skills. If fine or gross motor skill deficits are present, an occupational therapist will assess students. A physical therapist may evaluate students and measure their height and weight, observe them moving, test their balance and coordination, and do a hands-on assessment of muscle tone, flexibility, and strength. In cases where behavior is an issue, a behavior specialist may observe students or conduct a functional behavioral assessment (FBA).

> **DON'T FORGET**
> ....
> A psychological assessment is one piece of the overall assessment. The goal is to conduct a comprehensive assessment so that teachers and parents have a good understanding of a student's strengths and weaknesses.

Ability Level

When you receive a referral to evaluate students, it is a good idea to observe them in the classroom and talk to their teachers. Observations can provide some insight into the severity level of the disability. During this time, you should be thinking about your design for a test battery. Children may have mild, moderate, severe, or profound disabilities. Autism may be a possibility, or students may have one of the other problems discussed in

> **DON'T FORGET**
> ....
> Take notes when reading through a referral. You may need to follow up with questions for the teacher and/or parent.

Chapter 2. The issues that you observe and read about in the referral will have a direct impact on the assessment.

Test Availability

You may work in a school or residential setting that has a wide range of assessment measures. In this case, you can design a test battery, perhaps with limited restrictions, based on the areas you plan on assessing. But what if you work in a place with limited tests or outdated ones? In that case, your job has become more difficult. You may need to borrow tests from a larger school district in the area, if you have an established working relationship with another district. If you do not have such a relationship, you should develop one. Although it is best to have your own test kits, sometimes borrowing may be your only option. Many rural districts and financially poor districts do not have good test libraries. Practitioners working in these districts may have to be creative when designing test batteries.

Do not use old tests if new ones have been published in the last few years. Because of the Flynn effect, which we addressed in Chapter 5, tests scores from older tests may be inflated. Consequently, scores from these tests could prevent a student from being eligible for an intellectual disability program. If you only have access to old tests, consider forming a partnership with a larger or financially stronger school district that has a bigger test library.

Also consider the psychometric properties of tests. Doing this requires reading the test manuals; *we highly encourage each of you to read through test manuals*. Most published tests have good validity and reliability, but some tests are better than others. You need to ensure that the tests you choose are actually good ones. The best way to find out this information is to read the excellent, unbiased reviews in *Mental Measurements Yearbook* (*MMY*; Carlson, Geisinger, & Jonson, 2014). The Buros Institute of Mental Measurement publishes this book every few years. Your local college or university library may have access to an online version of *MMY*.

Finally, consider the standardization qualities of a test. Again, doing this requires looking through test manuals. How many students were included in the standardization? How many students with an intellectual disability were included? What about the ethnicities of the students? This information will help you to determine whether a test is appropriate to use with your particular student.

DON'T FORGET

Appendix C presents the *Guidelines to Professional Conduct* of the American Association on Intellectual and Developmental Disabilities (AAIDD) to help you to understand your responsibility to conduct appropriate assessments.

AREAS TO ASSESS

AAIDD (2010) described a conceptual framework of human functioning. This framework can be used in the design of a test battery. The framework includes five dimensions: intellectual ability, adaptive behavior, health, participation, and context. For the purposes of this chapter, we focus on the first two parts of this framework: *intellectual ability* and *adaptive behavior*. We also discuss a few other areas that should be assessed.

Intellectual Ability

Intelligence is multifaceted and is a major component of an intellectual disability assessment. Depending on your state's special education regulations, you may need to administer two intelligence tests and obtain two scores below 70 in order for the examinee to meet the intelligence requirement of intellectual disability eligibility. In most cases, you can use a test's confidence interval when looking at whether the scores fall below the 70 threshold. If a student has significant language problems or articulation problems that make him or her difficult to understand, consider using a nonverbal intelligence measure.

The assessment of intelligence is a very important part of an intellectual disability assessment. The results can be used to help determine an individual's level of functioning (i.e., mild, moderate, severe, profound). According to Tylenda and Brogan (2011, p. 5):

> All tests of cognitive ability are not alike. It is not enough to gain familiarity with one assessment measure and consistently use it in making a determination of intellectual disability. Intelligence tests may be normed on different populations, may have higher or lower levels of reliability and validity, may be based on different conceptual models of intelligence, and may access intelligence using different modalities (verbal, visual, kinesthetic, etc.). In the case of individuals with known or suspected cognitive impairments, these factors will need to be taken into account when choosing a diagnostic measure. The choice of test should be made such that an individual's performance on a given measure is maximized.

Rapid Reference 6.2 provides a list of traditional and nonverbal intelligence measures.

Rapid Reference 6.2 Intellectual Ability Assessment Measures

Test	Test Purpose	Ages	Testing Time	Publisher
Cognitive Assessment System—Second Edition (CAS2) (2014)	Measures cognitive processing abilities based on the PASS (Planning, Attention, Simultaneous, and Successive) cognitive/ neuropsychological theory	5–18:11	40–60 minutes	PRO-ED **Website:** http://www .proedinc.com
Comprehensive Test of Nonverbal Intelligence—Second Edition (CTONI–2) (2009)	Measures nonverbal intelligence	6–89:11	60 minutes	PRO-ED **Website:** http://www .proedinc.com
Differential Ability Scales—Second Edition (DAS–II) (2007)	General test of cognitive ability	2.6–17.11	45–60 minutes for the core battery; 30 minutes for the diagnostic subtests	Pearson **Website:** http://www .pearsonclinical.com
Kaufman Assessment Battery for Children— Third Edition (KABC–III) (2016)	General test of cognitive ability	3–18	25–70 minutes	Pearson **Website:** http://www .pearsonclinical.com
Naglieri Nonverbal Ability Test—Second Edition (NNAT2) (2011)	Nonverbal, culturally neutral assessment of general ability	4–18	30 minutes	Pearson **Website:** http://www .pearsonclinical.com
Primary Test of Nonverbal Intelligence (PTONI) (2008)	Assesses reasoning abilities in young children	3–9:11	5–15 minutes	PRO-ED **Website:** http://www .proedinc.com
Reynolds Intellectual Assessment Scales—Second Edition (RIAS–2) (2015)	General test of cognitive ability	3–90	20–40 minutes	PAR **Website:** http://www .parinc.com

Test	Test Purpose	Ages	Testing Time	Publisher
Stanford-Binet Intelligence Scales—Fifth Edition (SB5) (2003)	Assesses intelligence and cognitive abilities	2–89:9	15–50 minutes	Houghton Mifflin Harcourt Website: http://www.hmhco.com
Test of Nonverbal Intelligence—Fourth Edition (TONI–4)	Assesses aptitude, intelligence, abstract reasoning, and problem solving in a language-free format	6–89:11	15–20 minutes	PRO-ED Website: http://www.proedinc.com
Universal Nonverbal Intelligence Test—Second Edition (UNIT–2) (2015)	Measure of nonverbal intelligence Abbreviated Battery Standard Battery Full Scale Battery	5–21:11	10–60 minutes	PRO-ED Website: http://www.proedinc.com
Wechsler Adult Intelligence Scale—Fourth Edition (WAIS–IV) (2008)	General measure of intelligence for adolescents and adults	16–90:11	60–90 minutes	Pearson Website: http://www.pearsonclinical.com
Wechsler Intelligence Scale for Children—Fifth Edition (WISC–V) (2014)	General measure of intelligence for children and adolescents	6–16.11	60 minutes for the core battery	Pearson Website: http://www.pearsonclinical.com
Wechsler Nonverbal Scale of Ability (WNV) (2006)	Measure of nonverbal intelligence	4–21:11	15–20 minutes for the brief version; 45 minutes for the full battery	Pearson Website: http://www.pearsonclinical.com
Wechsler Preschool and Primary Scale of Intelligence—Fourth Edition (WPPSI–IV) (2012)	Measure of cognitive development in preschoolers and young children	2:6–7:7	30–45 minutes for ages 2:6–3:11; 45–60 minutes for ages 4:0–7:7	Pearson Website: http://www.pearsonclinical.com
Woodcock-Johnson IV Tests of Cognitive Abilities (WJ IV COG) (2014)	General measure of intelligence and cognitive abilities	2–90+	30–60 minutes	Houghton Mifflin Harcourt Website: http://www.hmhco.com

DON'T FORGET

Use the contact information in **Appendix A** to find out the specifics of intellectual disability special education eligibility criteria in your state.

Adaptive Behavior

Another major area in need of assessment is adaptive behavior. Adaptive behavior "is the collection of conceptual, social, and practical skills that have been learned and are performed by people in their everyday lives" (AAIDD, 2010, p. 15). Students with an intellectual disability typically have significant deficits in conceptual, social, and practical skills. In many cases, as these children move into adolescence and eventually adulthood, these deficits can prevent them from being fully independent. According to Reschly et al. (2002): "The domains assessed by adaptive behavior scales, and thus the individual items included on them, depend in part on the context, target age group, and purpose of the measure." These measures also can be used to help determine the level of impairment (i.e., mild moderate, several, and profound). See AAIDD's Technical Standards for Adaptive Behavior Assessment Instruments in **Rapid Reference** 6.3.

≡ Rapid Reference 6.3 AAIDD's Technical Standards for Adaptive Behavior Assessment Instruments (AAIDD, 2010)

- Focus on identifying significant limitations in adaptive behavior for the diagnosis of an intellectual disability.
- Assess specific dimensions that have emerged from factor-analytic studies of adaptive behavior that have indicated that the three primary areas of adaptive behavior are conceptual, social, and practical skills.
- Include measures of some aspects of adaptive behavior that are not currently measured by existing standardized instruments. These aspects include naiveté, gullibility (i.e., wariness), and technology-based skills.
- Contain items that maximally differentiate between individuals with and without an intellectual disability.

- Use item response theory to reliably measure individual levels of performance across the continuum of adaptive skills and ages, with special attention to providing precise information around the cutoff point for determining significant limitations in adaptive behavior.
- Allow the interviewer to probe further those items whose scoring influence the behavior's expression.
- Use an interviewer who is a professional (e.g., psychologist, case manager, social worker), one who has training in assessment and direct work experience with people with intellectual disability, and one who has had previous assessment experience.
- Use respondents who know the individual being assessed very well and have had the opportunity to observe the person on a daily or weekly basis in a variety of community settings and over an extended period of time. Respondents should be adults and may be selected from family members, friends, teachers, coworkers, employers, direct-support staff, case managers, or other adults who meet the above criteria.

DON'T FORGET

....

Obtain adaptive behavior rating scales from multiple sources.

Adaptive behavior rating skills are used to obtain feedback from parents, caregivers, teachers, and employers. We discuss some of the major rating scales in Chapter 8. It is important to obtain feedback from multiple sources. If a child has two parents, ask each parent to complete a rating scale. We have found that parents can differ in their viewpoint of a child's abilities. Parent rating scales also can yield scores higher than those from other sources. Parents may overestimate their child's ability, or they may not be able to compare their child to a child without adaptive behavior deficits as easily as a teacher can. The teacher spends time with students who do not have delays, but the parents may not; therefore, they may not have this perspective and may not readily see their child's deficits.

If adaptive scores from parents are inconsistent with a teacher scale and other information you have gathered, consider following up with an interview. You also may want to use another parent adaptive rating scale and administer it in an interview format. By questioning a parent and providing examples of what the item is asking, you may obtain feedback that more readily matches a child's deficits. State special education eligibility criteria may require that scores from an adaptive behavior scale be consistent with the child's intelligence; you do not want a high adaptive score from a parent to make it impossible for a child to qualify for services if the parent's responses does not match the child's adaptive skill level. So, be ready to conduct an interview should this happen in any of your cases. **Rapid Reference** 6.4 includes a list of measures of adaptive behavior that you can use during an intellectual disability assessment to assess an individual's conceptual, social, and practical skills. Scales that can help you to assess the intensity of support needs are also included.

Development and School Readiness

Students with an intellectual disability likely have delays in one or more areas of development. Rating scales are available to assess development in adaptive behavior, cognition, communication, motor development, and emotional development. As you can see, this area overlaps with other areas that we have discussed, which is good because it allows for multiple pieces of data for each student. A parent will complete a formal or informal measure of development. Parents can complete these scales independently, but they can also be interviewed and questioned for more information as they try to remember developmental milestones. If the child is older or has many siblings, the parent may have difficulty recalling certain information.

If a parent does not recall certain pieces of information, medical records can help to fill in the gaps. Assuming the child has seen the same pediatrician or family physician for a period of time, those records should contain historical data regarding development in addition to general medical information that could be helpful. In our experience, parents may forget or misremember information. **Rapid Reference** 6.5 provides a list of development and school readiness measures.

Academic Achievement

An evaluation should consist of an assessment of a student's academic achievement. Criterion- and norm-referenced tests of achievement may be used with students with or believed to have an intellectual disability. Tests can compare how a student is meeting district or state goals (criterion reference) or how a student compares to other students in the general population (norm reference). Achievement tests should assess reading, mathematics, and writing; some tests also may assess listening comprehension and oral expression. **Rapid Reference** 6.6 includes a list of achievement measures.

Rapid Reference 6.4 Adaptive Behavior and Supports Intensity Assessment Measures

Test	Test Purpose	Ages	Testing Time	Publisher
Adaptive Behavior Assessment System—Third Edition (ABAS–3) (2015)	Provides a complete assessment of adaptive skills across the life span	Birth–89	15–20 minutes	WPS **Website:** http://www.wpspublish.com
Adaptive Behavior Evaluation Scale—Revised Second Edition (ABES–R2) (2006)	Provides a measure of adaptive behaviors necessary for success in the educational and residential settings that are not measured by academic skills testing.	4-18	15-20 minutes	Hawthorne **Website:** http://www.hawthorne-ed.com
Diagnostic Adaptive Behavior Scale (DABS) (2016)	Provides a comprehensive standardized assessment of adaptive behavior	4–21	20–30 minutes	AAIDD **Website:** http://www.aaidd.org
Supports Intensity Scale—Children's Version (SIS–C) (2004)	Measures the relative intensity of support needs of children with intellectual disability	5–16	30–60 minutes	AAIDD **Website:** http://www.aaidd.org
Supports Intensity Scale—Adult Version (SIS–A) (2004)	Measures the relative intensity of support needs of people with intellectual disability	16 and above	30–60 minutes	AAIDD **Website:** http://www.aaidd.org
Vineland Adaptive Behavior Scales—Third Edition (Vineland–3) (2016)	Measures adaptive behavior from birth to adulthood	Birth–90	20–90 minutes for the Interview Form; 20 minutes for the Teacher Form	Pearson **Website:** http://www.pearsonclinical.com

Rapid Reference 6.5 Development and School Readiness Assessment Measures

Test	Test Purpose	Ages	Testing Time	Publisher
Battelle Developmental Inventory—Second Edition (BDI–2) (2004)	Screens and evaluates early childhood developmental milestones in these areas: personal-social, adaptive, motor, communication, and cognitive ability	Birth–7:11	10–30 minutes for the screening test; 60–90 minutes for the complete BDI–2	Houghton Mifflin Harcourt **Website:** http://www.hmhco .com
Bayley Scales of Infant and Toddler Development—Third Edition (Bayley–III) (2005)	Assesses different aspects of a young child's development in these areas: cognitive, motor, language, social-emotional, and adaptive behavior	1–42 months	10–15 minutes	Pearson **Website:** http://www .pearsonclinical.com
Bracken School Readiness Assessment—Third Edition (BSRA–3) (2007)	Quickly screens concept knowledge of young children	3:0–6:11	10–15 minutes	Pearson **Website:** http://www .pearsonclinical.com
Developmental Assessment of Young Children—Second Edition (DAYC–2) (2013)	Identifies children with possible delays in these domains: cognition, communication, social-emotional development, physical development, and adaptive behavior	Birth–5:11	10–20 minutes for each domain	Pearson **Website:** http://www .pearsonclinical.com
Developmental Profile—3 (DP–3) (2007)	Screen a child for developmental delays in five key areas: physical, adaptive behavior, social-emotional, cognitive, and communication	Birth–12:11	20–40 minutes	WPS **Website:** http:// www.wpspublish .com

85

Test	Test Purpose	Ages	Testing Time	Publisher
Riverside Early Assessments of Learning (REAL) (2013)	Addresses key areas of development and includes content tailored specifically for Head Start (orientation to learning, technology and engineering, language and literacy, cognitive and general knowledge, physical development and health, and social and emotional development); IDEA Parts B and C (academic, communication, motor, cognitive, adaptive, and personal-social), and Kindergarten Readiness (approaches to learning, cognitive and general knowledge, language and literacy development, physical development and health, and social and emotional development)	Birth—7:11	30 minutes	Houghton Mifflin Harcourt **Website:** http://www.hmhco.com
Woodcock-Johnson IV Tests of Early Cognitive and Academic Development (ECAD) (2015)	Assesses early cognitive and academic development	3–5; 6–9 for children with a cognitive or academic developmental delay	35 minutes for the core battery; 15 minutes for the extended battery	Houghton Mifflin Harcourt **Website:** http://www.hmhco.com

Rapid Reference 6.6 Achievement Assessment Measures

Test	Test Purpose	Ages	Testing Time	Publisher
Kaufman Test of Educational Achievement—Third Edition (KTEA–3) (2014)	Includes these subtests: Listening Comprehension, Oral Expression, Letter & Word Recognition, Reading Comprehension, Silent Reading Fluency, Reading Vocabulary, Nonsense Word Decoding, Phonological Processing, Associational Fluency, Object Naming Facility, Letter Naming Facility, Word Recognition Fluency, Decoding Fluency, Written Expression, Spelling, Writing Fluency, Math Concepts & Applications, Math Computation, and Math Fluency	4:0–25:11	15–85 minutes	Pearson **Website:** http://www .pearsonclinical .com
Wechsler Individual Achievement Test—Third Edition (WIAT–III) (2009)	Includes these subtests: Listening Comprehension, Early Reading Skills, Reading Comprehension, Math Problem Solving, Alphabet Writing Fluency, Sentence Composition, Word Reading, Essay Composition, Pseudoword Decoding, Numerical Operations, Oral Expression, Oral Reading Fluency, Spelling, Math Fluency—Addition, Math Fluency—Subtraction, and Math Fluency—Multiplication	4:0–50:11	Varies by grade level and number of subtests administered	Pearson **Website:** http://www .pearsonclinical .com
Wide Range Achievement Test 4 (WRAT4) (2006)	A quick measure of fundamental academic skills that includes these subtests: Math Computation, Spelling, Sentence Comprehension, and Word Reading	5–94	15–25 minutes for ages 5–7; 35–45 minutes for ages 8 and up	PAR **Website:** http://www .parinc.com

Test	Test Purpose	Ages	Testing Time	Publisher
Woodcock-Johnson IV Tests of Achievement, Forms A and B (WJ IV ACH) (2014)	Assesses achievement in four broad academic domains—reading, written language, mathematics, and academic knowledge—and includes these subtests: Letter-Word Identification, Applied Problems, Spelling, Passage Comprehension, Calculation, Writing Samples, Word Attack, Oral Reading, Sentence Reading Fluency, Math Facts Fluency, Writing Fluency, Reading Recall, Number Matrices, Editing, Word Reading Fluency, Spelling of Sounds, Reading Vocabulary, Science, Social Studies, and Humanities	2–90+	30–60 minutes	Houghton Mifflin Harcourt **Website:** http:// www.hmhco .com
Woodcock-Johnson IV Tests of Oral Language (WJ IV OL) (2014)	Useful for oral language assessment, determination of English (and Spanish) language proficiency, and includes these subtests: Picture Vocabulary, Oral Comprehension, Segmentation, Rapid Picture Naming, Sentence Repetition, Understanding Directions, Sound Blending, Retrieval Fluency, Sound Awareness, Vocabulario sobre dibujos, Comprensión oral, and Comprensión de indicaciones	2–90+	30–60 minutes	Houghton Mifflin Harcourt **Website:** http:// www.hmhco .com
Young Children's Achievement Test (YCAT) (2000)	Assists in the early identification of children at risk for school failure and includes these subtests: General Information, Reading, Writing, Mathematics, and Spoken Language	4:0–7:11	25–45 minutes	PRO-ED **Website:** http://www .proedinc.com

For initial evaluations, it is a good idea to assess all areas—basic reading, reading comprehension, math computation, math reasoning, and written expression. You also can administer reading fluency, math fluency, and/or writing fluency tests, but the results may not be as helpful. Students may not function well when being timed. If your concern is assessment of skills, skip the timed tasks.

For students already receiving special education services, standardized achievement scores are not likely to be very helpful. A better indicator of a student's ability is his or her progress toward meeting individualized education program (IEP) goals. You may still want to do an achievement test to see how scores compare to students in general. For the purpose of IEP goals, however, focus on the mastery of skills as listed in the IEP.

Behavior

Behavior rating scales have an important use in an intellectual ability assessment. If a student is displaying problematic behaviors, a behavior rating scale—completed by teachers, parents, caregivers, and others—can provide information about the severity of these behaviors. **Rapid Reference** 6.7 lists of broad behavior measures; many other measures assess specific areas, such as anxiety, depression, or self-concept. One thing to consider is that "the function of inappropriate or maladaptive behavior may be to communicate an individual's needs and, in some cases, may even be considered adaptive" (AAIDD, 2010, p. 49). Formal assessments allow assessors to find out which behaviors are significantly problematic, slightly problematic, or not problematic at all. Information from such an assessment may be used to generate interventions. In cases where the behavior is significant, a functional behavioral assessment (FBA) and behavior intervention plan (BIP) may be necessary.

A student may experience externalizing or internalizing behaviors, or both. Externalizing behaviors may include aggression, tantrums, fighting, or hyperactivity/impulsivity. Depression, anxiety, and withdrawal are examples of internalizing problems. More specialized rating scales for autism also may be used. As with adaptive behavior rating scales, it is good practice to ask more than one of the child's parents, if possible, to complete a rating scale. The parents may have very different opinions and insights about the behaviors.

Rapid Reference 6.7 Behavior Assessment Measures

Test	Test Purpose	Ages	Testing Time	Publisher
Achenbach System of Empirically Based Assessment (ASEBA) (2001)	Assesses adaptive and maladaptive functioning in children, adolescents, and adults	Teacher and Parent: 1.5–18; Self-Report: 11–59	30 minutes	Research Center for Children, Youth, and Families **Website:** http://www.aseba.org
Behavior Assessment System for Children—Third Edition (BASC–3) (2015)	Used to understand the behaviors and emotions of children and adolescents	Teacher and Parent: 2–21; Self-Report: 6–25	10–30 minutes	Pearson **Website:** http://www.pearsonclinical.com
Conners 3rd Edition (Conners 3) (2008)	Used to assess a wide range of behavior problems in children and adolescents	Teacher and Parent: 6–18; Self-Report: 8–18	10–20 minutes	Multi-Health Systems **Website:** http://www.mhs.com
Conners Comprehensive Behavior Rating Scales (Conners CBRS) (2008)	Provides a complete overview of child and adolescent concerns and disorders	Teacher and Parent: 6–18; Self-Report: 8–18	20 minutes	Multi-Health Systems **Website:** http://www.mhs.com
Emotional Disturbance Decision Tree (EDDT) (2010)	Assists in the identification of children who qualify for the special education category of emotional disturbance based on federal criteria	5–18	15–20 minutes	PAR **Website:** http://www4.parinc.com/

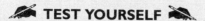

TEST YOURSELF

1. **Which area is not one of AAIDD's conceptual framework of human functioning?**
   (a) Intellectual ability
   (b) Adaptive behavior
   (c) Health
   (d) Socialization

2. **Which test would you choose if your theoretical approach aligned with the PASS (Planning, Attention, Simultaneous, and Successive) cognitive/neuropsychological theory?**
   (a) Woodcock-Johnson IV Tests of Cognitive Abilities
   (b) Wechsler Intelligence Scale for Children—Fifth Edition
   (c) Cognitive Assessment System—Second Edition
   (d) Differential Ability Scales—Second Edition

3. **Which nonverbal measure would you choose when working with a 3-year-old child?**
   (a) Primary Test of Nonverbal Intelligence
   (b) Wechsler Nonverbal Scale of Ability
   (c) Universal Nonverbal Intelligence Test—Second Edition
   (d) Comprehensive Test of Nonverbal Intelligence—Second Edition

4. **If you wanted to measures support requirements in 57 life activities and 28 behavioral and medical areas in a 17-year-old, which measure would you use?**
   (a) Vineland Adaptive Behavior Scales—Third Edition
   (b) Supports Intensity Scale—Children's Version
   (c) Adaptive Behavior Assessment System—Third Edition
   (d) Supports Intensity Scale—Adult Version

5. **You need to assess a child at birth. Which measure could you not use?**
   (a) Riverside Early Assessments of Learning
   (b) Developmental Profile–3
   (c) Battelle Developmental Inventory—Second Edition
   (d) Bayley Scales of Infant and Toddler Development—Third Edition

6. **Which measure is tailored specifically for Head Start, IDEA Parts B & C, and Kindergarten Readiness?**
   (a) Woodcock-Johnson IV Tests of Early Cognitive and Academic Development
   (b) Riverside Early Assessments of Learning
   (c) Bracken School Readiness Assessment—Third Edition
   (d) Developmental Assessment of Young Children—Second Edition

7. **Which measure can assess orientation to learning, technology and engineering, language and literacy, cognitive and general knowledge, physical development and health, and social and emotional development?**
   (a) Battelle Developmental Inventory—Second Edition
   (b) Riverside Early Assessments of Learning
   (c) Woodcock-Johnson IV Tests of Early Cognitive and Academic Development
   (d) Bracken School Readiness Assessment—Third Edition

8. **Which assessment instrument does not assess writing?**
   (a) Young Children's Achievement Test
   (b) Woodcock-Johnson IV Tests of Achievement
   (c) Kaufman Test of Educational Achievement—Third Edition
   (d) Wide Range Achievement Test 4

9. **Which test can be used to assess Spanish language proficiency?**
   (a) Wide Range Achievement Test 4
   (b) Woodcock-Johnson IV Tests of Oral Language
   (c) Woodcock-Johnson IV Tests of Achievement
   (d) Kaufman Test of Educational Achievement—Third Edition

10. **Which rating scale would not be appropriate if you wanted a teacher, parent, and student to complete a form?**
    (a) Conners 3rd Edition
    (b) Behavior Assessment System for Children—Third Edition
    (c) Achenbach System of Empirically Based Assessment
    (d) Emotional Disturbance Decision Tree

Answers: 1. B; 2. b; 3. d; 4. d; 5. d; 6. b; 7. d; 8. d; 9. b; 10. d

Seven

INTEGRATION OF ASSESSMENT RESULTS

Once you have gathered all of the information from the assessment, you need to write your psychological report. A report needs to be clear, concise, and reader-friendly. The report format can vary by practitioner, but, in general, a report includes several different components:

List of assessment procedures
Background information
Test interpretations
Summary
Recommendations

This chapter provides two brief sample reports: one for a student with a mild intellectual disability and one for a student with a moderate intellectual disability. For brevity, we include only the assessment procedures, background information, and test interpretations sections. Note that these reports are offered only as examples; your school or organization may dictate the actual report format required. You may need to follow certain requirements in regard to what you include in your report and how you interpret the information.

REPORT SAMPLE #1

Student: John Miller, Age 8, Grade 3, Mild Intellectual Disability

Assessment Procedures

Woodcock-Johnson IV Tests of Cognitive Abilities
Wechsler Intelligence Scale for Children—Fifth Edition
Woodcock-Johnson IV Tests of Achievement
Behavior Assessment System for Children—Third Edition: Teacher Rating
  Scales

Behavior Assessment System for Children—Third Edition: Parent Rating Scales
Adaptive Behavior Assessment System—Third Edition: Teacher Form
Adaptive Behavior Assessment System—Third Edition: Parent Form
Vision and hearing screenings (passed)
Records Review

Background Information

John was referred for a psychoeducational reevaluation to assist in determining his continued eligibility for special education services. He currently receives services for a significant developmental delay.

Parent Interview and Report. Barbara Miller, John's mother, says that he lives with his parents and a 4-year-old sister, Elizabeth. According to his mother, John has allergies and requires regular over-the-counter medication. Mrs. Miller described his vision as normal or near normal and his hearing as normal. At night, John typically sleeps soundly for 7 or 8 hours.

During pregnancy, John's mother had no significant health problems, and his delivery was normal. John's mother remembers him as a fussy, colicky, and irritable infant and toddler. His early motor skills, such as sitting up, crawling, and learning to walk, developed later than for most other children. His early language skills developed adequately.

DON'T FORGET
....
It can be very helpful to interview both parents since one parent may forget something or may remember events differently from the other.

DON'T FORGET
....
You want to ask the teacher not only how the child compares to another child with an intellectual disability but also how the child compares to same-age peers who are developing normally.

John attended preschool starting at age 4. He seemed to learn things with more difficulty than his same-age peers. His social skills were poor at times. According to his mother, John's behavior was very difficult to manage during his preschool years. Mrs. Miller reports that John currently demonstrates overactive and inattentive behaviors at home. He also demonstrates slightly serious uncooperative behavior and withdrawal.

Teacher Interview and Report. Teresa Brown, one of John's teachers, said that he needs more one-to-one attention and completes less schoolwork than most boys his age. Mrs. Brown says that John frequently fails to give close attention to details or makes careless mistakes. He often does not follow through on instructions and fails to finish his work. John often avoids, dislikes, or is reluctant to engage in tasks that are difficult for him. Mrs. Brown is most concerned about the way John responds to academic tasks requiring sustained mental effort; she believes this seriously impairs his classroom performance.

Test Results/Interpretations

Intelligence

Woodcock-Johnson IV Tests of Cognitive Abilities	
Cluster	Standard Score
General Intellectual Ability (GIA)	64 – Very Low

The **Woodcock-Johnson IV Tests of Cognitive Abilities** is a norm-referenced measure of cognitive ability. An average standard score is 100; 90 to 110 represents the Average range. Results indicate that John's General Intellectual Ability, or his overall level of intelligence, falls in the Very Low range.

> **DON'T FORGET**
> ....
> A bell curve can be a good visual to help parents understand how their child compares to the general population.

Wechsler Intelligence Scale for Children—Fifth Edition	
Composite Score	Standard Score
Full Scale IQ	**67 – Extremely Low**
Verbal Comprehension	62 – Extremely Low
Visual Spatial	72 – Borderline
Fluid Reasoning	70 – Borderline
Working Memory	71 – Borderline
Processing Speed	68 – Extremely Low

The **Wechsler Intelligence Scale for Children—Fifth Edition** is a norm-referenced measure of cognitive ability. An average standard score is 100; 90 to 109 represents the Average range. John's overall intelligence, as indicated by the Full Scale IQ, falls in the Extremely Low range.

Achievement

Woodcock-Johnson IV Tests of Achievement

Area	Subtest	Standard Score
Basic Reading	Letter-Word Identification	58 – Very Low
	Word Attack	66 – Very Low
Reading Comprehension	Passage Comprehension	70 – Low
Math Calculation	Calculation	72 – Low
Math Reasoning	Applied Problems	70 – Low

The **Woodcock-Johnson IV Tests of Achievement** is a norm-referenced measure of achievement that is designed to assess achievement in several important areas. An average score is 100; 90 to 110 represents the average range.

Reading: The Letter-Word Identification subtest requires the student to identify letters and/or read aloud individual words correctly. John's performance falls in the Very Low range. The Word Attack subtest requires the student to produce the sounds for single letters. John's performance falls in the Very Low range. The Passage Comprehension subtests requires student to demonstrate their understanding of symbolic learning or read a short passage and identify a missing key word that makes sense in the context of the passage. John's performance falls in the Low range.

Math: The Calculation subtest requires the student to perform mathematical computations. John's performance falls in the Low range. The Applied Problems subtest requires the student analyze and solve math problems. John's performance falls in the Low range.

Social-Emotional/Behavioral

Behavior Assessment System for Children—Third Edition: Teacher Rating Scales

Area	T-Score
Externalizing Problems	**69 +**
Hyperactivity	71 ++
Aggression	71 ++
Conduct Problems	59
Internalizing Problems	**71 ++**
Anxiety	61 +
Depression	81 ++
Somatization	56
School Problems	**76 ++**
Attention Problems	66 +
Learning Problems	82 ++

Behavior Assessment System for Children—Third Edition: Teacher Rating Scales

Area	T-Score
Behavioral Symptoms Index	**79 ++**
Atypicality	83 ++
Withdrawal	74 ++
Adaptive Skills	**26 ++**
Adaptability	24 ++
Social Skills	30 ++
Leadership	33 +
Study Skills	27 ++
Functional Communication	29 ++

+ = At Risk / ++ = Clinically Significant

The **Behavior Assessment System for Children—Third Edition: Teacher Rating Scales** is designed to facilitate the differential diagnosis and classification of a variety of emotional and behavioral disorders of children. Teresa Brown completed the teacher version of this measure. T-scores between 40 and 60 are average. Scores in the Clinically Significant range suggest a high level of maladjustment. Scores in the At-Risk range may identify a significant problem that may not be severe enough to require formal treatment or may identify the potential of developing a problem that needs careful monitoring.

Based on Ms. Brown's responses, John is perceived to be experiencing significant problems with hyperactivity, aggression, depression, learning, atypical behavior, withdrawal, adaptability, social skills, study skills, and functional communication. He is also perceived to be at risk for problems with anxiety, attention, and leadership skills.

Behavior Assessment System for Children—Third Edition: Parent Rating Scales

Area	T-Score
Externalizing Problems	**54**
Hyperactivity	65 +
Aggression	51
Conduct Problems	47
Internalizing Problems	**62 +**
Anxiety	51
Depression	72 ++
Somatization	55
Behavioral Symptoms Index	**79 ++**
Atypicality	75 ++
Withdrawal	90 ++
Attention Problems	77 ++

Behavior Assessment System for Children—Third Edition: Parent Rating Scales

Area	T-Score
Adaptive Skills	**20 ++**
Adaptability	20 ++
Social Skills	29 ++
Leadership	32 +
Activities of Daily Living	24 ++
Functional Communication	19 ++

+ = At Risk / ++ = Clinically Significant

Barbara Miller completed the parent version of the **Behavior Assessment System for Children—Third Edition: Parent Rating Scales**. T-scores between 40 and 60 are average. Scores in the Clinically Significant range suggest a high level of maladjustment. Scores in the At-Risk range may identify a significant problem that may not be severe enough to require formal treatment or may identify the potential of developing a problem that needs careful monitoring.

Based on Mrs. Miller's responses, John is perceived to be experiencing significant problems with depression, atypical behavior, withdrawal, attention, adaptability, social skills, activities of daily living, and functional communication. He is also perceived to be at risk for problems with hyperactivity and leadership skills.

Adaptive Behavior

Adaptive Behavior Assessment System—Third Edition

Composite	Standard Score	
	Teresa Brown, Teacher	Barbara Miller, Parent
Conceptual	51 – Extremely Low	52 – Extremely Low
Social	54 – Extremely Low	60 – Extremely Low
Practical	48 – Extremely Low	55 – Extremely Low
General Adaptive Composite	**45 – Extremely Low**	**51 – Extremely Low**

The **Adaptive Behavior Assessment System—Third Edition** is a checklist measure with forms completed by both parent and teacher to assess adaptive behavior skills in ten areas. Scaled scores of 7 through 13 are considered average; adaptive composites below 70 indicate significant deficits in adaptive behavior functioning. Teresa Brown completed the Teacher Form; Barbara Miller completed the Parent Form.

The General Adaptive Composite (GAC) measures the overall adaptive functioning of an individual. Its score is taken from all skill areas assessed. John's overall adaptive skills were rated as being Extremely Low in both the school and home settings.

The Conceptual Composite score consists of the following skill areas: Communication, Functional Academics, and Self-Direction. The Communication skill area assesses how well one speaks using appropriate grammar. It also looks at the ability one has to state information about oneself and how well one converses with others. Functional Academics assesses how well one performs the basics in academics in order to function daily at school, home, and the community. Self-Direction is assessed as how well one acts responsibly. For example, this can include completing schoolwork and chores, controlling anger and frustrations appropriately, and making responsible choices in spending money. John's adaptive skills were rated as being Extremely Low in both the school and home settings.

The Social Composite score is taken from two different skill areas: Leisure and Social. Leisure includes things one does when not in school or doing chores at home. Examples could include the following: reading a book or putting together a puzzle, playing games with friends, joining in sports activities, and/or joining some type of club. Social involves the ability to make friends and maintain friendships. It also assesses how well one is aware of other people's feelings and appropriate actions taken in certain situations. John's adaptive skills were rated as being Extremely Low in both the school and home settings.

The Practical Composite score is measured by four different skill areas: Community Use, Home Living, Health and Safety, and Self-Care. Community Use assesses how well one functions in the community. For example, this can include things like using the library and mailing letters at the post office. Home Living assesses how well one is able to do things at home for oneself. Making the bed, preparing food for oneself, and washing one's dishes are all examples of this skill area. Health and Safety is an important skill in that it looks at one's ability to be healthy and safe in everyday situations. This may include things like following rules, using caution around a hot stove, and seeking help when someone is hurt. Self-Care assesses how well one functions in taking care of self. One must be able to do everyday things on one's own, such as dressing, bathing, and using the bathroom. John's adaptive skills were rated as being Extremely Low in both the school and home settings.

DON'T FORGET

If an individual spends a great deal of time in the community with the subject you are assessing, this person may have the knowledge to complete an adaptive behavior rating scale.

Summary

John is an 8-year-old male student in the third grade at Main Street Elementary. He was referred for a psychoeducational reevaluation to assist in determining his continued eligibility for special education services. John currently receives services for a significant developmental delay.

Current test results indicate that John is functioning intellectually within the very low/extremely low range on two intelligence measures. Processing tests indicate that John's performance falls in the borderline to very low/extremely low ranges. With regard to his achievement, John's performance is low and very low in all areas assessed. Behavior rating scales indicate that John's teacher perceives him as experiencing significant problems with hyperactivity, aggression, depression, learning, atypical behavior, withdrawal, adaptability, social skills, study skills, and functional communication. His mother perceives him as experiencing significant problems with depression, atypical behavior, withdrawal, attention, adaptability, social skills, activities of daily living, and functional communication. Significant adaptive behavior deficits are noted based on both teacher and parent report. John's adaptive skills are rated as extremely low.

> **DON'T FORGET**
> ....
> A report summary needs to be a good, but brief, summarization of all the information collected on the individual.

REPORT SAMPLE #2

Student: Jake Williams, Age 14, Grade 8, Moderate Intellectual Disability

Assessment Procedures

Woodcock-Johnson IV Tests of Cognitive Abilities
Wechsler Intelligence Scale for Children—Fifth Edition
Woodcock-Johnson IV Tests of Achievement
Behavior Assessment System for Children—Third Edition: Teacher Rating Scales
Behavior Assessment System for Children—Third Edition: Parent Rating Scales
Behavior Assessment System for Children—Third Edition: Self-Report of Personality

Adaptive Behavior Assessment System—Third Edition: Teacher Form
Adaptive Behavior Assessment System—Third Edition: Parent Form
Teacher's Checklist
Parent's Checklist
Vision and hearing screenings (passed)
Records Review

Background Information

Jake was referred for a psychoeducational reevaluation to assist in determining strengths and weaknesses and to provide further direction for educational strategies. He currently receives special education services for a moderate intellectual disability.

Parent Interview and Report. Amelia Williams, Jake's mother, indicated that he lives with her and two younger siblings (Taylor and Sarah). According to his mother, Jake is usually in good health and is physically fit. Ms. Williams described Jake's vision as normal or near normal when corrective lenses are worn; his hearing is normal. At night, he typically sleeps for 7 to 9 hours, sometimes waking up at least once or twice during the night.

During pregnancy, Jake's mother had no significant health problems. His delivery was normal. Immediately after birth, he was healthy. Jake's mother remembers him as a loving, active, and happy infant and toddler. His early motor skills, such as sitting up, crawling, and learning to walk, developed earlier than for most other children. Jake's early language development, such as first words, asking simple questions, and talking in sentences, seemed to be typical.

Jake attended preschool, beginning at age 4. His preschool cognitive development and social skills progressed normally. No atypical behavior management problems were recalled.

Ms. Williams described Jake as affectionate and sociable. He is usually happy, though his mood varies normally. Ms. Williams said that Jake likes some things about school but dislikes others. It seems like he doesn't try to succeed at schoolwork. He frequently fails to give close attention to details or makes careless mistakes. He seems to have difficulty organizing and sustaining attention during his tasks and play activities. Jake often does not follow through on instructions and fails to finish his homework. He often avoids, dislikes, or is reluctant to engage in tasks that are difficult for him.

Test Results/Interpretations

Intelligence

Woodcock-Johnson IV Tests of Cognitive Abilities

Cluster Area	Standard Score
General Intellectual Ability (GIA)	53 – Very Low

The **Woodcock-Johnson IV Tests of Cognitive Abilities** is a norm-referenced measure of cognitive ability. An average standard score is 100; 90 to 110 represents the Average range. Results indicate that Jake's General Intellectual Ability, or his overall level of intelligence, falls in the Very Low range.

DON'T FORGET

An individual may have scores in the mild intellectual disability range even though the overall intelligence suggests a moderate intellectual disability. If the scores are generally consistent and there are no significant discrepancies among them, the overall intelligence score is likely the best estimate of intellectual ability.

Wechsler Intelligence Scale for Children—Fifth Edition

Composite Score	Standard Score
Full Scale IQ	**52 – Extremely Low**
Verbal Comprehension	51 – Extremely Low
Visual Spatial	55 – Extremely Low
Fluid Reasoning	50 – Extremely Low
Working Memory	48 – Extremely Low
Processing Speed	53 – Extremely Low

DON'T FORGET

If an examinee has a significant language disorder, it may be best to administer a nonverbal test of intelligence.

The **Wechsler Intelligence Scale for Children—Fifth Edition** is a norm-referenced measure of cognitive ability. An average standard score is 100; 90 to 109 represents the Average range. Jake's overall intelligence, as indicated by the Full Scale IQ, falls in the Extremely Low range.

Achievement

Woodcock-Johnson IV Tests of Achievement

Area	Subtest	Standard Score
Basic Reading	Letter-Word Identification	58 – Very Low
	Word Attack	49 – Very Low
Reading Comprehension	Passage Comprehension	48 – Very Low
Math Calculation	Calculation	56 – Very Low
Math Reasoning	Applied Problems	44 – Very Low

The **Woodcock-Johnson IV Tests of Achievement** is a norm-referenced measure of achievement that is designed to assess achievement in several important areas. An average score is 100; 90 to 110 represents the average range.

Reading: The Letter-Word Identification subtest requires the student to identify letters and/or read aloud individual words correctly. Jake's performance falls in the Very Low range. The Word Attack subtest requires the student to produce the sounds for single letters. Jake's performance falls in the Very Low range. The Passage Comprehension subtests requires student to demonstrate their understanding of symbolic learning or read a short passage and identify a missing key word that makes sense in the context of the passage. Jake's performance falls in the Very Low range.

Math: The Calculation subtest requires the student to perform mathematical computations. Jake's performance falls in the Very Low range. The Applied Problems subtest requires the student analyze and solve math problems. Jake's performance falls in the Very Low range.

Social-Emotional/Behavioral

Behavior Assessment System for Children—Third Edition: Teacher Rating Scales

	T-Score	
Area	Denise Buckley	Nancy Watkins
Externalizing Problems	**56**	**45**
Hyperactivity	65 +	47
Aggression	49	43
Conduct Problems	55	49
Internalizing Problems	**46**	**45**
Anxiety	47	45
Depression	49	47
Somatization	44	48

Behavior Assessment System for Children—Third Edition: Teacher Rating Scales

Area	T-Score Denise Buckley	Nancy Watkins
School Problems	**66 +**	**58**
Attention Problems	65 +	56
Learning Problems	65 +	58
Behavioral Symptoms Index	**53**	**52**
Atypicality	50	62 +
Withdrawal	43	51
Adaptive Skills	**41**	**38 +**
Adaptability	47	43
Social Skills	41	38 +
Leadership	41	35 +
Study Skills	37 +	42
Functional Communication	45	42

+ = At Risk / ++ = Clinically Significant

The **Behavior Assessment System for Children—Third Edition: Teacher Rating Scales** is an integrated system designed to facilitate the differential diagnosis and classification of a variety of emotional and behavioral disorders of children and to aid in the design of treatment plans. Denise Buckley and Nancy Watkins completed the teacher version of this measure. T-scores between 40 and 60 are average. Scores in the Clinically Significant range suggest a high level of maladjustment. Scores in the At-Risk range may identify a significant problem that may not be severe enough to require formal treatment or may identify the potential of developing a problem that needs carefully monitoring. Based on the two teachers' responses, no significant problems are noted; however, Jake is perceived to be at risk for problems with hyperactivity, attention, learning, atypical behavior, social skills, leadership skills, and study skills.

DON'T FORGET

Areas that are clinically significant may need some intervention. At the very least, the individual should be monitored.

Behavior Assessment System for Children—Third Edition: Parent Rating Scales

Area	T-Score
Externalizing Problems	**45**
Hyperactivity	46
Aggression	48
Conduct Problems	40

Behavior Assessment System for Children—Third Edition: Parent Rating Scales

Area	T-Score
Internalizing Problems	**51**
Anxiety	50
Depression	52
Somatization	47
Behavioral Symptoms Index	**47**
Atypicality	40
Withdrawal	47
Attention Problems	60 +
Adaptive Skills	**43**
Adaptability	52
Social Skills	44
Leadership	40 +
Activities of Daily Living	33 +
Functional Communication	47

+ = At Risk / ++ = Clinically Significant

Amelia Williams completed the parent version of the **Behavior Assessment System for Children—Third Edition: Parent Rating Scales**. T-scores between 40 and 60 are average. Scores in the Clinically Significant range suggest a high level of maladjustment. Scores in the At-Risk range may identify a significant problem that may not be severe enough to require formal treatment or may identify the potential of developing a problem that needs careful monitoring. Based on Ms. Williams's responses, no significant problems are noted; however, Jake is perceived to be at risk for problems with attention and activities of daily living.

Behavior Assessment System for Children—Third Edition: Self-Report of Personality

Area	T-Score
School Problems	**50**
Attitude to School	68 +
Attitude to Teachers	48
Sensation Seeking	35
Internalizing Problems	**52**
Atypicality	68 +
Locus of Control	61 +
Social Stress	42
Anxiety	45
Depression	57
Sense of Inadequacy	53
Somatization	41

Behavior Assessment System for Children—Third Edition: Self-Report of Personality

Area	T-Score
Inattention/Hyperactivity	**58**
Attention Problems	68 +
Hyperactivity	50
Emotional Symptoms Index	50
Personal Adjustment	**44**
Relations with Parents	32 +
Interpersonal Relations	52
Self-Esteem	58
Self-Reliance	40 +

+ = At Risk / ++ = Clinically Significant

Jake completed the self-report version of the **Behavior Assessment System for Children—Third Edition: Self-Report of Personality**. T-scores between 40 and 60 are average. Scores in the Clinically Significant range suggest a high level of maladjustment. Scores in the At-Risk range may identify a significant problem that may not be severe enough to require formal treatment or may identify the potential of developing a problem that needs careful monitoring. Based on Jake's responses, no significant problems are noted; however, he is perceived to be at risk for problems with his attitude toward school, atypical behavior, locus of control, attention problems, relations with parents, and self-reliance.

CAUTION

You may need to read a rating scale to an individual if reading ability and reading comprehension are deficits.

Adaptive Behavior

Adaptive Behavior Assessment System—Third Edition

Composite	Standard Score	
	Nancy Watkins, Teacher	Amelia Williams, Parent
Conceptual	53 – Extremely Low	56 – Extremely Low
Social	49 – Extremely Low	51 – Extremely Low
Practical	50 – Extremely Low	48 – Extremely Low
General Adaptive Composite	**51 – Extremely Low**	**54 – Extremely Low**

The **Adaptive Behavior Assessment System—Third Edition** is a checklist measure with forms designed to be completed by both parent and teacher to assess adaptive behavior skills in ten areas. Scaled scores of 7 through 13 are considered average; adaptive composites below 70 indicate significant deficits in adaptive behavior functioning. Nancy Watkins completed the Teacher Form; Amelia Williams completed the Parent Form. (Denise Buckley also completed the Teacher Form, but the form could not be scored because she indicated that she guessed at too many items.)

The General Adaptive Composite (GAC) measures the overall adaptive functioning of an individual. Its score is taken from all skill areas assessed. Jake's overall adaptive behavior is perceived to be Extremely Low based on teacher and parent report.

The Conceptual Composite score consists of the following skill areas: Communication, Functional Academics, and Self-Direction. The Communication skill area assesses how well one speaks using appropriate grammar. It also looks at the ability one has to state information about oneself and how well one converses with others. Functional Academics assesses how well one performs the basics in academics in order to function daily at school, home, and the community. Self-Direction is assessed as how well one acts responsibly. For example, this can include completing schoolwork and chores, controlling anger and frustrations appropriately, and making responsible choices in spending money. Jake's adaptive behavior is perceived to be Extremely Low based on teacher and parent report.

The Social Composite score is taken from two different skill areas: Leisure and Social. Leisure includes things one does when not in school or doing chores at home. Examples could include the following: reading a book or putting together a puzzle, playing games with friends, joining in sports activities, and/or joining some type of club. Social involves the ability to make friends and maintain friendships. It also assesses how well one is aware of other people's feelings and appropriate actions taken in certain situations. Jake's adaptive behavior is perceived to be Extremely Low based on teacher and parent report.

The Practical Composite score is measured by four different skill areas: Community Use, Home Living, Health and Safety, and Self-Care. Community Use assesses how well one functions in the community. For example, this can include things like using the library and mailing letters at the post office. Home Living assesses how well one is able to do things at home for oneself. Making the bed, preparing food for oneself, and washing one's dishes are all examples of this skill area. Health and Safety is an important skill in that it looks at one's ability in being healthy and safe in everyday situations. This may include things like following rules, using caution around a hot stove, and seeking help when someone is hurt. Self-Care assesses how well one functions in taking care of self. One must be able to do everyday things on one's own, such as dressing, bathing, and using the bathroom. Jake's adaptive behavior is perceived to be Extremely Low based on teacher and parent report.

Summary

Jake is a 14-year-old male student in the eighth grade at Main Middle School. He was referred for a psychoeducational reevaluation to assist in determining strengths and weaknesses and to provide further direction for educational strategies. He currently receives special education services for a moderate intellectual disability.

Current test results indicate that Jake's overall intellectual functioning falls within the very low/extremely low range on two different measures. Processing tests indicate that all of Jake's score are in the very low/extremely low range. With regard to his achievement, Jake's performance is low average in written expression, basic reading, reading fluency, and math calculation; it is low in reading comprehension and math reasoning. Behavior rating scales indicate that no significant problems are noted based on teacher, parent, or self-report. Jake's overall adaptive behavior is perceived to be extremely low based on teacher and parent report.

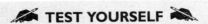 TEST YOURSELF

1. **An individual with a IQ of 58 would fall in which category of intellectual disability?**
   (a) Mild
   (b) Moderate
   (c) Severe
   (d) Profound

2. **On the Behavior Assessment System for Children—Third Edition, a T-score of 69 on any of the internalizing or externalizing problems subscales is considered:**
   (a) average.
   (b) at risk.
   (c) clinically significant.
   (d) either b or c, depending on the age of the individual.

3. **Communication, Functional Academics, and Self-Direction combine to form which composite on the Adaptive Behavior Assessment System—Third Edition?**
   (a) Practical
   (b) Social
   (c) Inhibitory
   (d) Conceptual

4. **A General Intellectual Ability score on the Woodcock-Johnson IV Tests of Cognitive Abilities that falls in the mild intellectual disability range would be considered:**
   (a) extremely low.
   (b) borderline.
   (c) very low.
   (d) limited.

5. **Letter-Word Identification and Word Attack comprise which cluster on the Woodcock-Johnson IV Tests of Achievement?**
   (a) Reading Foundations
   (b) Basic Reading
   (c) Advanced Reading
   (d) Reading Fundamentals

6. **The Full Scale IQ on the Wechsler Intelligence Scale for Children—Fifth Edition is made up of which five composites?**
   (a) Comprehension—Knowledge, Perceptual Reasoning, Working Memory, Processing Speed, Visual Spatial
   (b) Visual Processing, Long-Term Retrieval, Verbal Comprehension, Working Memory, Processing Speed
   (c) Short-Term Working Memory, Processing Speed, Fluid Reasoning, Verbal Comprehension, Visual Processing
   (d) Fluid Reasoning, Processing Speed, Verbal Comprehension, Visual Spatial, Working Memory

7. **The Behavior Assessment System for Children—Third Edition: Parent Rating Scales for a 14-year-old student includes which subtests in its Internalizing Problems scale?**
   (a) Anxiety, Withdrawal, Depression
   (b) Atypicality, Withdrawal, Depression
   (c) Anxiety, Depression, Somatization
   (d) Depression, Anxiety, Atypicality

Answers: 1. a; 2. b; 3. d; 4. c; 5. b; 6. d; 7. c

Eight

POSTASSESSMENT PLANNING

The chapter addresses the topic of providing feedback and guidance/ direction to parents of children and adolescents diagnosed with an intellectual disability (ID), and for caregivers/advocates of adults seeking community and vocational support services. For some parents, assessment findings may result in denial and a lack of acceptance of the assessment results, diagnosis, and/or prognosis. The chapter discusses the stages that parents may go through when their child receives such a diagnosis and the importance of allowing parents adequate time to process this information. The chapter also provides helpful guidelines for locating and accessing community-based resources, necessary information required for successful transition planning (including vocational skill development), and helpful hints on interventions for specific problems, such as providing clear expectations and guidelines for behavioral problems. Finally, the chapter addresses job-training opportunities for adults with an intellectual disability and the support services available to foster skills in independent living and self-advocacy.

The National Information Center for Children and Youth with Disabilities (NICHCY) website provides a wealth of information and resources for parents, educators, and anyone who wishes to obtain greater disability awareness (http://www.parentcenterhub.org/nichcy-resources/). One important article posted on this website is an informative message about "Parenting a Child with Special Needs" (NICHCY, 2003). Although the article was not written specifically for parents of children with intellectual disabilities, the information in the article definitely provides an overview of the "unexpected journey" parents begin when they learn that their child has a disability or serious illness. NICHCY publishes articles in the *News Digest* to address the many questions that those involved with children with special needs may have. Parents are often confronted with difficult decisions and choices in their interactions with a number of different professionals and specialists that may be involved in their child's case. Often parents may be overwhelmed and feel isolated and alone on their quest to seek out information and support. Parents of a child with a newly diagnosed disability may be in shock and denial when they first are given the news; others need help at transition points along the path when the direction changes (transition to secondary school, transition to vocational planning, etc.).

COMMON PARENT REACTIONS TO LEARNING A CHILD HAS A DISABILITY

Written by a parent of a child with a disability, "You Are Not Alone" (Smith, 2003) discusses common emotional experiences that parents go through when they first learn that their child has a disability. Two of the most common initial reactions are *denial* ("This can't be true") followed by *anger* (usually toward the individuals who have introduced the diagnosis). Anger can be complex because it is often triggered by feelings of *grief* for and *loss* of the "normal child" that was. *Fear* is another common emotion that parents experience at this time when they begin to think about how this will alter the future for their child and fear that they may not be able to provide what is necessary for the child to succeed in life. Fear of the unknown often results from not fully understanding the disability or fearing the potential worst of outcomes for the child and the potential consequences for other family members (siblings, grandparents, etc.). Fear is also a common reaction to expectations of the child being discriminated against or not totally being accepted by society.

Among the kaleidoscope of emotions is *guilt*, with parents often questioning if there was something they could have done to prevent this from happening or something they did that caused it to happen. Many parents will experience feelings of *confusion* because they are overwhelmed with all these mixed feelings, which make it difficult to make choices or make decisions based on integrating information from different sources; this further adds to the frustration. A sense of *powerlessness* often overcomes parents when they feel the situation is out of their control and that they are helpless to change anything. In the newness of the circumstances, parents may not know where to turn or whom to trust.

Along with initial feelings of grief and loss, parents also often feel a profound sense of *disappointment* as they look into an uncertain future. Finally, many parents feel guilty for experiencing feelings of *rejecting* their "special needs" child and longing for the "ideal" child that was to be. All these emotional reactions are normal and often accompany experiencing a new diagnosis but may resurface at important transition points or if the disability takes on more serious consequences.

GUIDELINES FOR PARENTS OF INDIVIDUALS WITH DEVELOPMENTAL DISABILITIES

In 2003, *News Digest* published a series of articles for parents with children who have special needs. In addition to outlining the many emotions that are triggered by the diagnosis of a disability, the publication also provided suggestions to help parents on their journey. Smith (2003) suggests several avenues that are available to parents to assist in coping with the diagnosis, including:

- Seeking the assistance of another parent who is farther along in the journey. The National Information Center for Children and Youth with Disabilities (NICHCY) lists parent groups that parents can contact for assistance.
- Talking to family members to enlist their support.
- Seek out positive influences (pastor, counselor) to help with the overwhelming emotions that are experienced.
- Stay focused on the day-to-day possibilities rather than dwell on future potential disasters.
- Get better acquainted with the terminology used by the various systems and professionals.
- Stay informed and reading to provide you with background information and controversial issues in the area.
- Don't be intimidated and be free to ask important questions.
- Find programs that will enhance your child's potential for success.

In their contribution to the articles appearing in the *News Digest*, Brown, Goodman, and Kupper (2003) suggested several guidelines for parents whose children have been diagnosed with developmental disorders, including:

- Gather and compile information about your child's disability, assessment reports, and other important information (available services) so that you will better understand and be able to share this information with other sources (e.g., school system).
- Locate and join a parent group that advocates for your child's disability.
- Find materials written by other parents who have children with similar disabilities. (As always, be careful, since information from the internet can be unreliable or undocumented. Be sure to frequent credible sources, such as NICHCY.)
- Find out about services in your area for children within your child's age range. Families with children from birth through 3 years of age should access *early intervention services* to obtain immediate support. For school-aged children with disabilities, special education services can be an important way to address your child's needs.

TRANSITION PLANNING

As we discussed in Chapter 3, children undergo several important transitions during the developmental period, which are monitored by the education system. Important transitions include transitions from services provided prior to the age of three to services that are available for children 3 through 21 years of age. During these times, children will transition from elementary school to middle school; from middle school to secondary school; and finally, to postsecondary education, employment, and independent living. During this time frame, children and adolescents up to 21 years of age are legally entitled to a free appropriate public education (FAPE) in the least restrictive environment (LRE) through special education and related services. These services are provided until receipt of a high school diploma or the end of the school year of the student's 21st birthday, whichever is earlier.

Transition services must be included in all individual education programs (IEPs) once a child reaches 16 years of age. The term "transition services" refers to a coordinated set of activities for a child with a disability that focuses on making transitions seamless by facilitating movement from school to postschool activities, including: postsecondary education; vocational education; integrated employment, including supported employment; any continuing and adult education programs; adult services; independent living arrangements; or community participation programs. If needed, daily living skills and functional vocational evaluation may also be included.

Levels of Severity and Expected Levels of Functioning

The needs of individuals with intellectual disabilities can vary widely depending on the level of severity and the existence of any comorbid disorders or accompanying physical disabilities. However, the vast majority (85%) of those with an intellectual disability will be considered to have a mild level of severity (IQ range approximately 50–70). For individuals in this category, academic expectations will likely peak at a sixth-grade level (APA, 2000). Individuals with a mild intellectual disability can be successful in vocational settings with minimal support or supervision; however, if under stressful conditions or if the rules change, they may not be able to adapt without additional support or assistance. Approximately 10% of individuals with an intellectual disability will have a moderate level of severity (IQ 35–50 range). They would experience less success academically and would be at the level of attaining the equivalent of a second-grade education. Individuals at this category would be able to function in sheltered workshops or be capable of completing highly structured tasks with minimal supervision. Behavioral methods can be very helpful in providing structured programmed instruction for teaching social and vocational skills.

As the degree of severity of an intellectual disability increases, there is increasing likelihood that the individual will also be at risk for medical, neurological, and motor problems. Approximately 3% to 4% of individuals with an intellectual disability will have a severe intellectual disability (IQ in the 20–35 range). Individuals in this category will be capable of mastering only very basic preacademic skills, often requiring significant repetition in order to consolidate learning. Long-range plans often involve living in group home settings where they can be closely monitored. Individuals who have a profound degree of an intellectual disability (IQ of 20 and below) are the most compromised, often due to significant neurological impairment, and represent approximately 1% to 2% of all those with an intellectual disability. Long-term placements would be most likely to include sheltered settings where they can be closely monitored. Often medical care is required and some system of augmentative communication (e.g., picture boards) may be needed in order to communicate their needs to others.

The Arc: Assistance in Transition Planning

The Arc has lobbied for the rights of individuals with an intellectual disability for the past 60 years. The Arc works to protect people with intellectual and developmental disabilities and their families on the federal level through public policy initiatives and has almost 700 state and local chapters that provide resources and services for individuals with an intellectual disability and their families. On their website (http://www.thearc.org), The Arc lists the nature of the supports and services that are offered by The Arc chapters including:

- information and referral services.
- individual advocacy to address education, employment, health care, and other concerns.
- self-advocacy initiatives.
- residential support.
- family support.
- employment programs.
- leisure and recreational programs.

Additional services that may also be available, such as: early intervention; supported employment; job training; transition planning; respite care; supported living; case management; medical and dental care; and therapeutic services, such as occupational and physical therapy, behavior management, speech therapy, and more. The website also provides a link to find the nearest/local chapter.

SELF-DETERMINATION AND INDIVIDUALS WITH DEVELOPMENTAL DISABILITIES

Field, Martin, Miller, Ward, and Wehmeyer (1998, p. 2) defined self-determination as:

> a combination of skills, knowledge, and beliefs that enable a person to engage in goal-directed, self-regulated, autonomous behavior. An understanding of one's strengths and limitations, together with a belief in oneself as capable and effective are essential to self-determination. When acting on the basis of these skills and attitudes, individuals have greater ability to take control of their lives and assume the role of successful adults in our society.

The concept of self-determination has been increasingly applied to the delivery of services in education and vocational settings for individuals with developmental disabilities. There are several reasons for this, including increased emphasis on quality of life and independent living and civil rights movements to ensure that individuals with disabilities are free from discrimination (e.g., the Americans with Disabilities Act Amendments Act [ADAAA] of 2008). Furthermore, research evidence that adults with disabilities are at increased risk of being unsuccessful in their employment efforts or in meeting adequate standards of living and independence has provided increased momentum on the need to develop a positive sense of self-determination in these individuals (Ward, 1996).

DON'T FORGET

....

You can read The Arc's position statement on self-determination in **Appendix D**.

Shogren (2013) examined the contextual factors inherent in the acquisition of self-determination behavior in order to provide a framework for the development and design of supports that can enhance self-determination in individuals with developmental disabilities. Shogren used Bronfenbrenner's (1989) ecological model to provide an overarching framework for the set of interrelated systems that influence human growth and development. Bronfenbrenner's model was built on a series of concentric circles beginning with the individual at the core and moving out from the center to include influences that involve several systems, including the: *microsystem* (immediate environment, including family, peers) *exosystem* (school and community), and *macrosystem* (culture and society).

The important thing to recognize with the system is that the directions of influence are bidirectional and that the system is considered to be ecological and transactional in nature. Based on her literature review, Shogren (2013) suggested a number of variables that can be subsumed under the circles of influence envisioned in Bronfenbrenner's model. The characteristics are summarized in **Rapid Reference** 8.1.

≡ Rapid Reference 8.1 Ecological Characteristics of Self-Determination

Level of Influence	Factors	Characteristics
MICROSYSTEM	Individual	Disability label
		Age
		Gender
		Race ethnicity
		Culture
	Family Factors	Promote and value self-determination
	Social Networks	Social skills and self-determination
EXOSYSTEM	School Factors	Teacher characteristics/training
		School programs/access to general education/inclusion
		Opportunities for self-determination?
		IEP meetings
	Disability Support System	Transition to life programs
		Collaboration between programs
	Community Factors	Community engagement
		Community leisure activities
MACROSYSTEM	Cultural Norms/Beliefs	Cultural concept of disability
	Public Policy	Emphasis on self-determination and practice

Within the *microsystem,* Shogren (2013) provided research evidence that individuals with lower cognitive capacity report lower levels of self-determination. Additionally, findings in her research with other colleagues (Shogren et al., 2007) suggested that female adolescents with disabilities may have higher ratings for self-determination compared to males with disabilities. Research also has found that family beliefs and the promotion of self-determination is higher in families whose children do not have special needs compared to those who do have children with special needs, and in families where parents have achieved higher levels of education. Socially, the relationship between social skills and self-determination has also been investigated, with results suggesting that inclusion of peers with and without disabilities in a social network can enhance self-determination in both groups.

The next level of influence is the *exosystem*, which includes influences from factors such as schools, disability support systems, and community factors. In this sector, emphasis has not only been on how to increase self-determination in children with developmental disabilities but also on how to be instrumental in removing barriers to self-determination and autonomy. Within this context, teacher training and time allotted to provide opportunities for self-determination can be major factors in how these characteristics are successfully integrated into the educational system. For youth with disabilities, active participation in the IEP meeting has been predictive of higher levels of self-determination.

Finally, at the outermost level of influence is the *macrosystem*, which involves influences of culture, beliefs, and public policies or the law. Cultures vary in their attitudes and beliefs about disabilities and their reluctance or acceptance of support from outside sources. Shogren (2103) firmly believed that "when policies are developed that promote valued outcomes, such as self-determination, practice is shaped by these policies and future policies are shaped by the outcomes of these practices" (p. 502).

APPLICATION OF SELF-DETERMINATION PRACTICES

Research to Practice in Self-Determination is a series of training exercises based on research in the area of self-determination. The series of papers discusses "key issues in the field of developmental disabilities that can be enhanced by considering efforts to promote self-determination" (Calkins, Jackman, & Beckman, 2011, p. 1). One area that is thought to be instrumental to self-determination is the role of self-advocacy. Calkins, Jackman, and Beckman (2011) defined self-advocacy as "a set of behaviors that enable people with developmental disabilities to speak out or demonstrate their preferences in a way that promotes their needs and desires or those of a collective group to assure their access to and full participation in the community" (p. 3). According to Calkins et al., self-determination is inextricably tied to self-advocacy since it includes the rights and ability to advocate for "choosing and setting goals, being involved in making life decisions, self-advocating, and working to reach goals," ultimately leading to "attainment of more positive outcomes, such as employment, education, community living, and an enhanced quality of life" (p. 3).

Calkins and colleagues (2011) share a similar perspective with Shogren (2013) when they discuss self-advocacy and self-determination within a social ecological framework, which they consider to be "particularly useful as one considers building social capital in the context of self-advocacy—formal and informal support networks that help an individual have greater resources in the community" (p. 4). Calkins et al. (2011, p. 4) discuss four self-advocacy skills that can lead to enhanced self-determination: assertiveness, rights and responsibilities, communication, and leadership. Each of the four skills is defined in the following way

Self-advocacy Skill	Description
Assertiveness	Ability to communicate an opinion and defend rights in a way that enhances mutual respect and minimizes potential conflict.
Rights and responsibilities	Expressing one's rights the core element of assertive behavior. Therefore, people should know their rights and the accompanying responsibilities.
Communication	Includes conversation skills, listening skills and body language skills. Developing these skills enhances the ability to be a self-advocate.
Leadership	Leaders guide or direct others on a course of action, influence the opinions and behaviors of others, and show the way by going in advance.

The Research to Practice in Self-Determination document contains several sections that deal with various issues facing individuals with developmental disabilities and provides sources of information and guidance on how to address the issues and concerns. Some of the suggestions are summarized next.

Use of Lifebooks

The lifebook technique has been used by social workers and adoptive parents to develop a life story based on pictures, stories, and memorabilia of a child's life prior to adoption. Eversman (2011) suggested that this technique could be an important venue for collecting information about significant events in the lives of children with developmental disabilities to assist caregivers and support providers with future issues of self-advocacy. Eversman suggested that the exercise of creating the lifebook itself can be rewarding and create a bonding experience in several ways:

- The focus of the exercise is on the individual with special needs and his or her unique story.
- The exercise can involve family and friends and discussions about the past and future.
- The information can be helpful to support staff and can assist them in getting to know the individual better.
- The lifebook can be used in therapy to assist the individual with the disability to better understand the disorder in the context of their environment and supports.
- Involvement in creating a lifebook can inspire the individual to become more involved in his or her own life planning.
- Hunley (2011) contends that through Linux, it is possible for individuals with disabilities to afford the assisted technology they will need.

The Use of Assisted Technology

Hunley (2011) addresses the need for increased access to assisted technology for individuals with developmental disabilities. Although most individuals are concerned with prohibitive pricing of such services, Hunley introduced the Linux system, which is a free, open-access, and open-source technological resource. According to Hunley, "A variety of assistive technology software is available through Linux, including: interaction applications, text-to-speech, screen readers, screen magnifiers, gesture recognition, head tracking, and many others" (p. 12). As an example, Hunley described a system that is specifically designed for "those with visual challenges, is called Vinux." According to their website (http://vinux.org.uk), "Vinux is 'optimized for visually impaired users. It provides a screen-reader, full-screen magnification and support for Braille displays out of the box'" (p. 12).

Self-Advocacy Online

The Arc has partnered with the Research and Training Center on Community Living (RTC) at the University of Minnesota in the support and development of an online website developed specifically for individuals with an intellectual disability to assist in developing skills in self-advocacy. The website is located at http://www.selfadvocacyonline.org. The program, developed by RTC, provides a number of multimedia lessons on topics such as "living self-determined, healthy, contributing lives in their communities." The website includes videos of individuals sharing their stories and contains a list of local and national self-advocacy groups. The site also shares research and pertinent data and information about an intellectual disability in a way that is easily accessible to individuals with an intellectual disability. In addition, you can read a position statement on self-advocacy for individuals with an intellectual and/or developmental disability, written as a collaboration between the American Association on Intellectual and Developmental Disabilities and The Arc, in **Appendix E**.

RESULTS OF THE ARC SURVEY: FINDS 2011

In 2011, results of the Family and Individual Needs for Disability Supports (FINDS) survey was published online on The Arc website (http://www.thearc .org/document.doc?id=3672). The survey was conducted between July and October of 2010 and was disseminated online through a number of supportive associations, including the Association of University Centers on Disabilities, the American Association on Intellectual and Developmental Disabilities, the American Network of Community Options and Resources, the National Association of Councils on Developmental Disabilities, Self-Advocates Becoming Empowered, the National Council on Independent Living, Best Buddies, Easter Seals, the Autism Society of America, and state and local chapters of The Arc. Responses were received from individuals with disabilities from 38 states and the District of Columbia. The respondents included 4,962 caregivers and 558 individuals with disabilities. This summary presents highlights of that report, titled "Still in the Shadows with Their Future Uncertain: A Summary of Key Findings and a Call to Action." The article was published on the 50th anniversary of President Kennedy's "Call to Action" for improved conditions for individuals with an intellectual disability. Despite obvious gains in recognition, rights, education, and living conditions, the FINDS (2011) report outlined several areas where outcomes still fall short of what they should be for opportunities for individuals with an intellectual disability in education, employment, funding, and support services. Some of the reported survey results include the following:

- 52% left secondary school without a high school diploma; 10% never finished high school.
- 8% report having any college experience.
- Less than one-third of those with an intellectual disability are fully included in primary/middle schools (29%) or high schools (32%).

- Four out of 10 parents reported dissatisfaction with the quality of educational programming for students in primary/middle school (40%) or high school (38%).
- 85% of families reported their adult children with an intellectual disability are unemployed, full or part time.
- One out of five families (20%) report that someone in the family had to quit their job to stay home and support the needs of their family member with an intellectual disability.
- More than 75% of families report they cannot find afterschool care, non-institutional community services, trained reliable home care providers, summer care, residential, respite, and other services.
- 62% of families reported that services were being cut in the community, limiting or eliminating access to community life and opportunities for their family member with an intellectual disability.
- 43% of families reported that schools had cut back on services, such as physical, occupational or speech therapies.
- 32% of parents/caregivers reported that they were on waiting lists for government-funded services, with the average wait more than five years. They were waiting for personal assistance, respite care, housing, therapy, employment supports, transportation, and more.

The report states that although progress has certainly been made, funding has taken a recent downturn due to the recession. As a result, individuals with intellectual and developmental disabilities and their families have been among the hardest hit. While the report recognized that many barriers have been removed from education and employment for individuals with an intellectual disability, many individuals have not yet seen their potential realized. But the report also recognized the great progress that has been made in several areas.

In addition to the many hardships in supports, employment, and education, families also reported that:

- Compared to earlier times of segregation and isolation, today 98% of people with an intellectual disability live in the community, with 78% living with family members, 9% in group homes of six or fewer people, and 7% in their own homes or apartments;
- Compared to earlier days of institutionalization, 83% to 86% of people with an intellectual disability attended public school, while 12% to 14% attended private school and 3% were homeschooled, depending on the level of school (e.g. primary, middle, or high school);

- 84% of family members believed that it was important for their family member with an intellectual disability to continue their education after high school or go back to school as an adult to learn a job-related skill (73%), to learn about things they are interested in (72%), to have experiences that will help them get a job (66%), as well as other reasons.
- While only 15% are employed, either full time or part time, those that have a job are happy with what they do (82%) and with their work hours (78%).

The report concluded on a very positive note and a call to action for continued improvement in the quality of education, employment, and living standards for individuals with an intellectual disability. You can read position statements written by The Arc on education (**Appendix F**) and employment (**Appendix G**) for individuals with an intellectual and/or developmental disability.

DON'T FORGET

Appendix H provides a list of helpful websites.

🖋 TEST YOURSELF 🖋

1. **Two of the most common initial reactions that parents experience when they learn that their child has a disability include:**
   (a) Guilt and confusion.
   (b) Anger and grief/loss.
   (c) Powerlessness and confusion.
   (d) Disappointment and rejection.

2. **Brown, Goodman, and Kupper (2003) suggest several guidelines for parents whose children have been diagnosed with developmental disorders, including:**
   (a) Gather and compile information about your child's disability, assessment reports, and other important information (available services).
   (b) Locate and join a parent group that advocates for your child's disability.
   (c) Find materials written by other parents who have children with similar disabilities.
   (d) All of the above.

3. **Eighty-five percent of those with an intellectual disability will have a mild degree of severity and can likely achieve what level of education?**
   (a) Grade 2
   (b) Grade 8
   (c) Grade 6
   (d) Grade 4

4. **Under IDEA, individuals with disabilities are entitled to receive a free and appropriate education in the least restrictive environment:**
   (a) Until the end of the school year they reach 21 years of age or obtain a high school diploma.
   (b) Until they reach 18, or the age of majority.
   (c) As long as they desire to continue their lifelong learning.
   (d) As long as they can demonstrate a need for further education or training.

5. _____ **is defined as a combination of skills, knowledge, and beliefs that enable a person to engage in goal-directed, self-regulated, autonomous behavior.**
   (a) Self-advocacy
   (b) Self-determination
   (c) Self-efficacy
   (d) Self-concept

6. **According to Shogren (2013), family influences and individual characteristics that contribute to the development of self-determination comprise what level of Bronfenbrenner's ecological model?**
   (a) Mesosystem
   (b) Macrosystem
   (c) Microsystem
   (d) Exosystem

7. **Calkins et al. (2011, p. 4) discuss four self-advocacy skills that can lead to enhanced self-determination. Which of the following is not one of those skills?**
   (a) Leadership
   (b) Rights and responsibilities
   (c) Communication
   (d) Aggressiveness

8. **With regard to education and employment and individuals with an intellectual disability, the FINDS survey (2011) reported that:**
   (a) 52% left secondary school without a high school diploma.
   (b) more than half of children with an intellectual disability were educated in general education classes.
   (c) 70% were unemployed.
   (d) 10% of parents reported dissatisfaction with the quality of education their child received.

Answers: 1. b; 2. d; 3. c; 4. a; 5. b; 6. c; 7. d; 8. A

Appendix A

State Departments of Special Education

Alabama Department of Special Education

50 North Ripley Street
Montgomery, AL 36104
334-242-9700

http://alex.state.al.us/specialed/

Alaska Department of Special Education

801 W. Tenth Street, Suite 200
Juneau, AK 99801
907-465-2972

https://education.alaska.gov/tls/sped/

Arizona Department of Exceptional Student Services

1535 West Jefferson Street, Bin 24
Phoenix, AZ 85007
602-542-4013

http://www.azed.gov/special-education/

Arkansas Department of Special Education

1401 West Capitol Avenue, Suite 450
Little Rock, AR 72201
501- 682-4221

http://arksped.k12.ar.us/

California Special Education Division

1430 N. Street, Suite 2401
Sacramento, CA 95814
916-445-4613

http://www.cde.ca.gov/sp/se/

Colorado Exceptional Student Leadership Unit

1560 Broadway, Suite 1175
Denver, CO 80202
303-866-6694

http://www.cde.state.co.us/cdesped

Connecticut Bureau of Special Education

P.O. Box 2219
Hartford, CT 06145
860-713-6912

http://www.sde.ct.gov/sde/site/default.asp

Delaware Exceptional Children Group

401 Federal Street, Suite 2
Dover, DE 19901
302-735-4000

http://www.doe.k12.de.us/Page/183

Department of Defense Education Agency Office of Special Education

4040 North Fairfax Drive
Arlington, VA 22203
703- 588-3147

http://www.dodea.edu/Curriculum/specialEduc/

Florida Bureau of Exceptional Education and Student Services

325 West Gaines Street, Suite 614
Tallahassee, FL 32399
850-245-0475

http://www.fldoe.org/academics/exceptional-student-edu/index.stml

Georgia Office of Standards, Instruction and Assessment - Exceptional Students

1870 Twin Towers East
Atlanta, GA 30334
404-656-3963

http://www.gadoe.org/Curriculum-Instruction-and-Assessment/Special-Education-Services/Pages/default.aspx

Hawaii Special Education Services Branch

475 22nd Avenue, Room 115
Honolulu, HI 96816
808-203-5560

http://www.hawaiipublicschools.org/TeachingAndLearning/SpecializedPrograms/SpecialEducation/Pages/home.aspx

Idaho Department of Special Education

650 West State Street
Boise, ID 83720
208-332-6911

http://www.sde.idaho.gov/site/special_edu/

Illinois Department of Special Education Services

100 N. First Street
Springfield, IL 62777
217-782-4321

http://www.isbe.net/SPEC-ED/DEFAULT.HTM

Indiana Office of Special Education

151 West Ohio Street
Indianapolis, IN 46204
317-232-0570

http://www.doe.in.gov/specialed

Iowa Department of Special Education

400 E 14th Street
Des Moines IA 50319
515-281-5294

https://www.educateiowa.gov/pk-12/special-education

Kansas Department of Special Education Services

120 SE 10th Avenue
Topeka, KS 66612
800-203-9462

http://www.ksde.org/Agency/DivisionofLearningServices/EarlyChildhood
SpecialEducationandTitleServices/SpecialEducation.aspx

Kentucky Division of Exceptional Children Services

500 Mero Street, 8th Floor CPT
Frankfort, KY 40601
502-564-4970

http://education.ky.gov/specialed/excep/pages/default.aspx

Louisiana Division of Special Populations

1201 North 3rd Street
Baton Rouge, LA 70804
225-342-3730

https://www.louisianabelieves.com/academics/students-with-disabilities

Maine Department of Special Services

23 State House Station
Augusta, ME 04333
207-624-6600

http://www.maine.gov/doe/specialed/

Maryland Division of Special Education/Early Intervention Services

200 West Baltimore Street, 9th Floor
Baltimore, MD 21201
410-767-0238

http://www.marylandpublicschools.org/MSDE/divisions/earlyinterv/

Massachusetts Department of Special Education

75 Pleasant Street
Malden, MA 02148
781-338-3000

http://www.doe.mass.edu/sped/

Michigan Office of Special Education and Early Intervention Services

608 W. Allegan Street
Lansing, MI 48909
517-373-0923

http://www.michigan.gov/mde/0,1607,7-140-6530_6598---,00.html

Minnesota Division of Special Education

1500 Highway 36 West
Roseville, MN 55113
651-582-8614

http://education.state.mn.us/MDE/SchSup/SpecEdComp/

Mississippi Office of Special Education

359 North West Street, Suite 301
Jackson, MS 39205
601-359-3498

http://www.mde.k12.ms.us/OSE

Missouri Division of Special Education

P.O. Box 480
Jefferson City, MO 65102
573-751-5739

https://dese.mo.gov/special-education

Montana Department of Special Education

P.O. Box 202501
Helena, MT 59620
406-444-3095

http://opi.mt.gov/Programs/SpecialEd/

Nebraska Office of Special Education

301 Centennial Mall South
Lincoln, NE 68509
402-471-2471

http://www.education.ne.gov/sped/

Nevada Department of Special Education, Elementary and Secondary Education, and School Improvement

700 E. Fifth Street
Carson City, NV 89701
775-687-9200

http://www.doe.nv.gov/Office_of_Special_Education/

New Hampshire Bureau of Special Education

101 Pleasant Street
Concord, NH 03301
603-271-3494

http://education.nh.gov/instruction/special_ed/

New Jersey Office of Special Education Programs

P.O. Box 500
Trenton, NJ 08625
609-292-0147

http://www.nj.gov/education/specialed/

New Mexico Special Education Bureau

120 South Federal Place, Room 206
Santa Fe, NM 87501
505-827-1457

http://www.ped.state.nm.us/seb/

New York Office of Vocational and Educational Services for Individuals with Disabilities

One Commerce Plaza, Room 1606
Albany, NY 12234
518-474-3852

http://www.p12.nysed.gov/specialed/

North Carolina Exceptional Children Division

301 N. Wilmington Street, 6th Floor
Raleigh, NC 27601
919-807-3300

http://ec.ncpublicschools.gov

North Dakota Department of Special Education

600 E. Boulevard Avenue
Bismarck, ND 58505
701-328-2260

https://www.nd.gov/dpi

Ohio Office of Exceptional Children

25 South Front Street
Columbus, OH 43215
877-644-6338

http://education.ohio.gov/Topics/Special-Education

Oklahoma Department of Education

2500 North Lincoln Boulevard
Oklahoma City, OK 73105
405-522-3248

http://www.ok.gov/sde/special-education

Oregon Special Education Unit

255 Capitol Street, NE
Salem, OR 97301
503-947-5782

http://www.ode.state.or.us/search/results/?id=40

Pennsylvania Bureau of Special Education

333 Market Street, 7th Floor
Harrisburg, PA 17126
717-783-6913

http://www.pde.state.pa.us/SPECIAL_EDU/site/default.asp

Rhode Island Office for Diverse Learners

255 Westminster Street
Providence, RI 02903
401-222-4600

http://www.ride.ri.gov/StudentsFamilies/SpecialEducation/Special
EducationRegulations.aspx

South Carolina Office of Exceptional Children

1429 Senate Street, Room 808
Columbia, SC 29201
803-734-8806

http://ed.sc.gov/districts-schools/special-education-services/

South Dakota Office of Educational Services & Support

700 Governors Drive
Pierre, SD 57501
605-773-3134

http://doe.sd.gov/oess/sped.aspx

Tennessee Division of Special Education

710 James Robertson Parkway
Nashville, TN 37243
615-741-2851

http://tn.gov/education/

Texas Special Education Unit

1701 North Congress Avenue
Austin, TX 78701
512-463-9414

http://tea.texas.gov/index2.aspx?id=2147491399

Utah Special Education Services Unit

250 E. 500 South
Salt Lake City, UT 84114
801-538-7587

http://www.schools.utah.gov/sars/

Vermont Department of Special Education

120 State Street
Montpelier, VT 05620
802-828-3135

http://education.vermont.gov/special-education

Virginia Division of Special Education and Student Services

P.O. Box 2120
Richmond, VA 23218
800-292-3820

http://www.doe.virginia.gov/special_ed/

Washington Special Education Section

600 Washington Street, S.E
Olympia, WA 98504
360-725-6000

http://www.k12.wa.us/specialed/

West Virginia Office of Special Programs, Extended and Early Learning

1900 Kanawha Boulevard
Charleston, WV 25305
304-558-2696

http://wvde.state.wv.us/osp/

Wisconsin Division for Learning Support: Equity and Advocacy

125 S. Webster Street
Madison, WI 53707
800-441-4563

http://sped.dpi.wi.gov

Wyoming Office of Special Education

320 West Main Street
Riverton, WY 82501
307-777-2555

http://edu.wyoming.gov/in-the-classroom/special-programs/

Appendix B

AAIDD and The Arc Position Statement on the Criminal Justice System

The following position statement was written as a collaboration between the American Association on Intellectual and Developmental Disabilities (AAIDD) (http://www.aaidd.org) and The Arc (http://www.thearc.org). It was approved by both organizations in 2014.

CRIMINAL JUSTICE SYSTEM

People with intellectual and/or developmental disabilities[1] (I/DD) have the right to justice and fair treatment in all areas of the criminal justice system, and must be afforded the supports and accommodations required to make justice and fair treatment a reality.

---

[1] "People with intellectual disability (ID)" refers to those with "significant limitations both in intellectual functioning and in adaptive behavior as expressed in conceptual, social, and practical adaptive skills. This disability originates before age 18," as defined by the American Association on Intellectual and Developmental Disabilities (AAIDD) in its manual, *Intellectual Disability: Definition, Classification, and Systems of Supports* (Schalock et al., 2010), and the *Diagnostic and Statistical Manual of Mental Disorders, 5th Edition* (DSM–5), published by the American Psychiatric Association (APA, 2013). "People with developmental disabilities (DD)" refers to those with "a severe, chronic disability of an individual that (i) is attributable to a mental or physical impairment or combination of mental and physical impairments; (ii) is manifested before the individual attains age 22; (iii) is likely to continue indefinitely; (iv) results in substantial functional limitations in 3 or more of the following areas of major life activity: (I) Self-care, (II) Receptive and expressive language, (III) Learning, (IV) Mobility, (V) Self-direction, (VI) Capacity for independent living, (VII) Economic self-sufficiency; and (v) reflects the individual's need for a combination and sequence of special, interdisciplinary, or generic services, individualized supports, or other forms of assistance that are of lifelong or extended duration and are individually planned and coordinated," as defined by the Developmental Disabilities Assistance and Bill of Rights Act 2000. In everyday language people with an intellectual disability and/or DD are frequently referred to as people with cognitive, intellectual and/or developmental disabilities.

Issue

When individuals with intellectual and/or developmental disabilities (I/DD) become involved in the criminal justice system as victims, witnesses, suspects, defendants, or incarcerated individuals, they face fear, prejudice, and lack of understanding. Attorneys, judges, law enforcement personnel (including school-based security officers), first responders, forensic evaluators, victim advocates, court personnel, correctional personnel, criminal justice policy-makers, and jurors may lack accurate and appropriate knowledge to apply standards of due process in a manner that provides justice for individuals with I/DD. These individuals are:

- *Unrecognized as having a disability.* Individuals with I/DD are frequently undiagnosed or misdiagnosed, especially by evaluators, including law enforcement personnel, who are not trained in assessment of individuals with intellectual disability and who do not recognize common characteristics such as individuals' attempts to hide their disability. Defendants with I/DD are often denied a fair evaluation of whether they are entitled to legal protection as having I/DD on the basis of false stereotypes about what individuals with I/DD can and cannot understand or do;
- *Victimized at high rates.* Individuals with I/DD are significantly more likely to be victimized (at least two times more likely for violent crimes and four to ten times for abuse and other crimes), yet their cases are rarely investigated or prosecuted because of discrimination, devaluation, prejudice that they are not worthy of protection, and mistaken stereotypes that none can be competent witnesses. Their victimization comes in many forms, including violence, oppression, financial exploitation, sexual exploitation, and human trafficking;
- *Denied redress.* Individuals with I/DD are subject to routine denial of opportunities for legal redress because of outdated and stereotyped views of their credibility, their competence to testify, or their need for advocacy, supports, and accommodations;
- *Denied due process.* Individuals with I/DD are often denied due process and effective, knowledgeable advocacy and legal representation at each stage of the proceedings; and
- *Discriminated against in sentencing, confinement, and release.* Individuals with I/DD are subject to abuse and exploitation when incarcerated and denied either alternatives to incarceration or appropriate habilitation programs that would address their intellectual disability, and/or behavior, and help them

return safely to the community. When incarcerated, individuals with I/DD often serve extended time because they do not understand or cannot meet steps to reduce time and secure an earlier release.

When individuals with I/DD or their families come into contact with the criminal justice system, they find few organized resources for information, training, technical assistance, referral, and supports. Moreover, people living with I/DD who enter the criminal justice system encounter unique problems not faced by their nondisabled peers, such as:

- Failing to have their disability correctly identified by authorities who lack the expertise to discern the presence and nature of their disability (especially when the disability is denied by the person or somewhat hidden);
- Giving incriminating statements or false "confessions" because the individual is manipulated, coerced, misled, confused by either conventional or inappropriately used investigative techniques, or desires to please the questioner;
- Experiencing inappropriate assessments for competency to stand trial even when the individual cannot understand the criminal justice proceeding or is unable to assist their lawyer in their own defense;
- Being inappropriately placed in long-term institutions and subject to inappropriate one-size-fits-all "competency training" designed for people with other disabilities or no disabilities; and
- "Waiving" rights unknowingly when warnings such as *Miranda* are given without accommodating the person's I/DD.

While the Supreme Court ruled in *Atkins v. Virginia*[2] that it is a violation of the Eighth Amendment ban on cruel and unusual punishment to execute people with intellectual disability, states continue to play a major role in applying the term and in deciding the process for consideration of a defendant's intellectual disability. Laws vary from state to state on how a defendant proves the presence of intellectual disability. States also vary widely regarding whether it is the judge or jury who

---

[2] *Atkins v. Virginia*, 536 U.S. 304 (2002). The term "mental retardation" was used in the *Atkins* decision banning execution of people with intellectual disability (ID) and, though outdated, was still used in some state legal and criminal justice systems until the U.S. Supreme Court's decision in *Hall v. Florida*. The outdated term has appeared, therefore, in many legal decisions and briefs, including amicus ("friend of the court") briefs. The Arc and AAIDD support the modern terminology of an intellectual disability and urge courts to follow the Supreme Court's lead in adopting this modern terminology.

decides if the defendant has intellectual disability. States sometimes inappropriately appoint people who are not knowledgeable about intellectual disability to conduct "assessments" for intellectual disability or to offer "a diagnosis" that they are not professionally trained or qualified to provide. As a result, defendants may not have their intellectual disability correctly identified because of a state's unfair and inaccurate procedures. The Supreme Court ruled again in *Hall v. Florida*[3] in 2014, reaffirming the *Atkins* decision and denying states' use of strict IQ cutoffs to diagnose intellectual disability.

Position

People with intellectual and/or developmental disabilities must receive justice in the criminal justice system, whether as victims, witnesses, suspects, defendants, or incarcerated individuals.

As victims, witnesses, suspects, defendants, or incarcerated individuals, they must:

- Be protected by laws and policies that ensure their right to justice and fair treatment;
- Be treated fairly by personnel who are knowledgeable and trained about I/DD, including all attorneys (prosecution and defense), judges, law enforcement personnel (including school-based security officers), first responders, forensic evaluators, victim advocates, court personnel, correctional personnel, criminal justice policy-makers, and jurors;
- Be informed about and have access to appropriate sentencing alternatives to incarceration, and be provided the supports and accommodations to enter alternatives;
- Receive supports and accommodations to effectively participate in all stages of legal proceedings for which they are competent;
- Have necessary supports and accommodations available so that their testimony is heard and fairly considered when they are victims;
- Have access to victim supports and compensation as appropriate;
- Have access to, and the right to present, expert evaluations and testimony by professionals with training, experience, and expertise in their disability;
- Have an advocate, in addition to their lawyer, who has specialized, disability-related expertise;
- Have their conversations with their advocate covered under, or treated similarly to, attorney-client privilege; and

---

[3] *Hall v. Florida*, 134 S. Ct. 1986 (2014).

- As a suspect, be protected from harm, self-incrimination, and exploitation at all stages of an investigation and prosecution, including when they are questioned, detained, and incarcerated.

When sentenced, individuals with I/DD also must:

- Have available reasonable and appropriate supports, accommodations, treatment, and education, as well as alternatives to sentencing and incarceration that include community-based corrections; and
- Have access to well-trained probation and parole officers who will treat them fairly based on their individual disability and their need for the supports and accommodations necessary to re-enter society, including those that will enable people to re-establish Medicaid Waiver services, SSI, housing, education, and job supports.

When death penalty is an issue, individuals with intellectual disability also must:

- Continue to be exempt from the death penalty because existing case-by-case determinations of competence to stand trial, criminal responsibility, and mitigating factors at sentencing have proved insufficient to protect the rights of individuals with intellectual disability;
- Have access to expert witnesses and professionals who are knowledgeable about, as well as trained and experienced in, intellectual disability and who can accurately determine the presence and effects of intellectual disability; and
- Have their intellectual disability determined by state procedures that are accurate and fair. Those state procedures must be consistent with the national standards on making an intellectual disability determination and ensure that people with intellectual disability are not executed.

Adopted:

American Association on Intellectual and Developmental Disabilities
Board of Directors
June 22, 2014
The Arc
Board of Directors
July 27, 2014
Chapters of The Arc
October 2, 2014

Source: http://www.thearc.org/who-we-are/position-statements/rights/criminal-justice

Appendix C

American Association on Intellectual and Developmental Disabilities (AAIDD)

Guidelines to Professional Conduct

POSITION STATEMENT OF AAIDD

Preamble

The American Association on Intellectual and Developmental Disabilities is a professional organization that advances the knowledge and skills of individuals in the field of intellectual disability and related developmental disabilities; strives to enhance the life opportunities of people with intellectual disability and their families; and promotes public policies, research, and services that advance individual choices and human rights. The Association has developed guidelines for professional conduct that offer a set of values, principles, and standards to guide practice.

Guidelines

1. The practitioner fosters effective communication first and foremost with the individual, using all possible alternative means of communication to ascertain his/her unique needs, values, and choices.
2. The practitioner objectively honors, respects, and upholds the unique needs, values, and choices expressed by the individual being served.
3. The practitioner communicates fully and honestly in the performance of his/her responsibilities and provides sufficient information to enable individuals being supported and others to make their own informed decisions to the best of their ability.
4. The practitioner protects the dignity, privacy, and confidentiality of individuals being supported and makes full disclosure about any limitations on his/her ability to guarantee full confidentiality.
5. The practitioner is alert to situations that may cause a conflict of interest or have the appearance of a conflict. When a real or potential conflict of

interest arises, the practitioner not only acts in the best interest of individuals being supported, but also provides full disclosure.

6. The practitioner seeks to prevent, and promptly responds to, signs of abuse and exploitation whether it is physical, mental, sexual, or financial in nature.

7. The practitioner engages neither in a dual relationship in which there is a professional and a personal relationship with the individual nor conduct that is abusive/exploitive in a physical, mental, sexual, or financial manner.

8. The practitioner assumes responsibility and accountability for personal competence in evidence-based practice and professional standards of his/her respective field, continually striving to increase professional knowledge and skills and to apply them in practice.

9. The practitioner exercises professional judgment within the limits of his/her qualifications and collaborates with others, seeks counsel, or makes referrals as appropriate.

10. The practitioner fulfills commitments in good faith and in a timely manner.

11. The practitioner conducts his/her practice with honesty, integrity, and fairness.

12. The practitioner provides services in a culturally competent manner and does not discriminate against individuals on the basis of race, ethnicity, religion, sex, age, sexual orientation, national origin, or disability.

13. The practitioner is diligent in being knowledgeable regarding changes and emerging trends in guiding philosophies within the field (e.g., self-determination, self-advocacy, inclusion), and ensures that his/her professional practices remain compatible.

14. The practitioner strives to use and educate others to use preferred terminology and people-first language, rather than perpetuate the use of outdated and offensive terms.

15. The practitioner maintains currency in research findings for evidenced-based practices and, when applicable, applies those findings to practice and where needed, advocates for inclusion of persons with intellectual disability in the discussion of the application of such findings.

Adopted:

AAIDD Board of Directors
July 11, 2012

Source: http://aaidd.org/news-policy/policy/position-statements/guidelines

Appendix D

The ARC Position Statement on Self-Determination

The following position statement on self-determination was written by The Arc (http://www.thearc.org) and approved by the organization in 2011.

SELF-DETERMINATION

People with intellectual and/or developmental disabilities (I/DD)[1] have the same right to, and responsibilities that accompany, self-determination as everyone else. They must have opportunities, respectful support, and the authority to exert control in their lives, to self-direct their services to the extent they choose, and to advocate on their own behalf.

Issue

Many individuals with intellectual and/or developmental disabilities have not had the opportunity or the support to make choices and decisions about important aspects of their lives. Instead, they are often overprotected and involuntarily segregated, with others making decisions about key elements of their lives. Many individuals with I/DD have not had the experiences that would enable them to learn decision-making skills, take more personal control in their lives, and make choices. The lack of such learning opportunities has impeded people with I/DD from becoming participating, valued, and respected members of their communities, living lives of their own choosing.

---

[1] "People with intellectual and/or developmental disabilities" refers to those defined by AAIDD classification and *DSM–IV*. In everyday language they are frequently referred to as people with cognitive, intellectual and/or developmental disabilities although the professional and legal definitions of those terms both include others and exclude some defined by *DSM–IV*.

Position

People with intellectual and/or developmental disabilities have the same right to self-determination as all people and must have the freedom, authority, and support to exercise control over their lives. To this end, they must:

In their personal lives have:

- opportunities to advocate for themselves with the assurance that their desires, interests, and preferences will be respected and honored.
- opportunities to acquire and use skills and knowledge which better enable them to exercise choice.
- the right to take risks.
- the right to choose their own allies.
- the lead in decision-making about all aspects of their lives.
- the option to self-direct their own supports and services and allocate available resources.
- the choice and support necessary to hire, train, manage, and fire their own staff.

In their community lives have:

- the right to receive the necessary support and assistance to vote.
- opportunities to be supported to become active, valued members and leaders of community boards, advisory councils, and other organizations.
- opportunities to take leadership roles in setting the policy direction for the self-determination movement.
- the right to representation and meaningful involvement in policy-making at the federal, state, and local levels.

Adopted:

Congress of Delegates, The Arc of the United States, 2011

Source: http://www.thearc.org/who-we-are/position-statements/rights/self-determination

Appendix E

AAIDD and The Arc Position Statement on Self-advocacy

The following position statement on self-advocacy was written as a collaboration between the American Association on Intellectual and Developmental Disabilities (AAIDD; http://www.aaidd.org) and The Arc (http://www.thearc.org). It was approved by both organizations in 2014.

SELF-ADVOCACY

People with intellectual and/or developmental disabilities[1] (I/DD) must have the right to and be supported to act as self-advocates. Self-advocates exercise their rights as citizens by communicating for and representing themselves, with supports in doing so, as necessary. This means they have a say in decision-making in all areas of their daily lives and in public policy decisions that affect them.

---

[1] "People with intellectual disability (ID)" refers to those with "significant limitations both in intellectual functioning and in adaptive behavior as expressed in conceptual, social, and practical adaptive skills. This disability originates before age 18," as defined by the American Association on Intellectual and Developmental Disabilities (AAIDD) in its manual, *Intellectual Disability: Definition, Classification, and Systems of Supports* (Schalock et al., 2010), and the *Diagnostic and Statistical Manual of Mental Disorders, 5th Edition* (*DSM–5*), published by the American Psychiatric Association (APA, 2013). "People with developmental disabilities (DD)" refers to those with "a severe, chronic disability of an individual that (i) is attributable to a mental or physical impairment or combination of mental and physical impairments; (ii) is manifested before the individual attains age 22; (iii) is likely to continue indefinitely; (iv) results in substantial functional limitations in 3 or more of the following areas of major life activity: (I) Self-care, (II) Receptive and expressive language, (III) Learning, (IV) Mobility, (V) Self-direction, (VI) Capacity for independent living, (VII) Economic self-sufficiency; and (v) reflects the individual's need for a combination and sequence of special, interdisciplinary, or generic services, individualized supports, or other forms of assistance that are of lifelong or extended duration and are individually planned and coordinated," as defined by the Developmental Disabilities Assistance and Bill of Rights Act 2000. In everyday language people with an intellectual disability and/or DD are frequently referred to as people with cognitive, intellectual and/or developmental disabilities.

Issue

Historically, people with I/DD have experienced powerlessness and isolation resulting in loss and denial of basic human rights, segregation, and discrimination in almost all areas of personal and community life.

Before self-advocacy groups existed, only a small number of people with I/DD received education and support from people who had experiences like their own. Without these groups they did not have a way to learn about important self-advocacy skills or topics like:

- Their rights and responsibilities as citizens, such as the right to vote;
- Development of leadership and assertiveness skills;
- Confidence in their own abilities;
- Using their expertise as people living with disabilities;
- Development of public speaking skills and problem-solving techniques, and involvement in group decision-making; and
- Involvement on boards and task forces and with policymakers at the local, state, and national level.

Without self-advocacy skills, people with I/DD have little impact on their own situations or on public policy that affects them.

Position

People with intellectual and/or developmental disabilities have the right to advocate for themselves. This means they have the right to speak or act on their own behalf or on behalf of other people with disabilities, whether the issue is personal (e.g., housing, work, friends) or related to public policy. Recognizing these rights in a respectful partnership between people with and without disabilities can lead to better outcomes and better lives in the community for everyone.

Self-advocates provide important knowledge, experience, and skills that individuals, organizations, and government agencies need in order to effectively support the needs and dreams of people with I/DD. To promote this participation, it is critical to acknowledge the important role that self-advocacy groups play in developing leadership skills and increasing people's pride, influence, and opportunities. To achieve this partnership between self-advocates and their support persons or organizations, the following must occur:

- People with I/DD must have the power to make day-to-day decisions about their own lives and the services they receive free from the manipulation of others. Service providers and government agencies can offer significant supports in making sure informed decision making is in the hands of the self-advocate.

- People with I/DD should be provided accommodations or supports in order to have a visible, respected, and meaningful place in meetings, conferences, task forces, or other forums when issues and policies that are important to them are discussed ("Nothing about us without us" principle). These accommodations may include, but not be limited to:
  - Extra time planned for meetings to accommodate the unique communication and participation needs of each person;
  - Enhanced and alternative communication methods with easy-to-use formats;
  - Communication devices, sign language or other similar accommodations;
  - Supporting people to serve as "translators"; and
  - Appropriate transportation and funding.
- Respectful communication is important when talking to or about people with I/DD. This includes using people first language whenever talking directly to someone with disabilities, or describing their lives, and speaking to them in a way that takes into account their unique communication abilities.
- Policy development by any entity at a local, state, or national level must include self-advocates in matters of governance, and periodically evaluate the effectiveness of that inclusion.
- People who provide direct support and disability advocates should work actively with people with I/DD to develop and sustain self-advocacy organizations and individual participants in their states and communities.
- Families, advocacy organizations, service providers, and government agencies must also work with self-advocates to increase public awareness of the importance of the self-advocacy movement and the need to support it.
- Foundations and federal, state, and local funding agencies must promote self-advocacy as a key matter of policy. These entities must provide enough money and resources to make sure that (1) people with I/DD have accessible information, training, and education in self-advocacy and (2) providers have the information they need to deliver services that match the self-advocate-led trends in policy and design.
- Families, schools, direct service providers, and other agencies must have the support they need to make sure that children and youth have the chance to learn self-advocacy skills and put them into practice. They should have opportunities to use those skills in educational planning (including

Individualized Education Programs, or IEPs, and transition plans) and all decision-making.

- Self-advocates, families, direct service providers, and other agencies must have the support they need to make sure that adults with I/DD have the chance to learn self-advocacy skills and put them into practice. They should have opportunities to use those skills in service planning and all decision-making.

Adopted:

American Association on Intellectual and Developmental Disabilities
Board of Directors
July 16, 2014

The Arc
Board of Directors
July 27, 2014

Chapters of The Arc
October 2, 2014

Source: http://www.thearc.org/who-we-are/position-statements/rights/self-advocacy

Appendix F

The ARC Position Statement on Education

The following position statement on education was written by The Arc (http://www.thearc.org) and approved by the organization in 2011.

EDUCATION

Children and youth with intellectual and/or developmental disabilities (I/DD)[1] must receive a free, appropriate public education as guaranteed by the Individuals with Disabilities Education Act (IDEA). Education must include individualized supports and services, quality instruction, and access to the general education curriculum in age-appropriate inclusive settings, in preparation for adult life.

Issue

IDEA requires that students with disabilities be educated to the maximum extent appropriate with students who do not have disabilities. However, many students with intellectual and/or developmental disabilities remain segregated in self-contained classrooms or separate schools, with few or no opportunities for academic or social involvement in inclusive settings. Students with I/DD frequently do not have access to quality instruction or services and supports necessary to participate as full members of their school communities. Consequently, many students with I/DD leave school unprepared for work, postsecondary education, or adult life in the community.

Administrators, educators, and support staff too often lack sufficient training and knowledge about the needs and abilities of these students. School districts struggle to recruit and retain qualified special education personnel.

---

[1] "People with intellectual and/or developmental disabilities" refers to those defined by AAIDD classification and *DSM–IV*. In everyday language they are frequently referred to as people with cognitive, intellectual and/or developmental disabilities although the professional and legal definitions of those terms both include others and exclude some defined by *DSM–IV*.

Paraprofessionals providing support in inclusive classrooms are often poorly paid and do not always receive or seek professional development relevant to students' needs.

Outdated, inaccurate beliefs about students with I/DD persist, leading to low expectations, segregated classrooms, and a diminished sense of accountability for these students. In some communities, No Child Left Behind's focus on student performance has led to the conclusion that these students are "bringing down" test scores and are to blame when schools and school systems do not achieve adequate yearly progress.

Position

Students with intellectual and/or developmental disabilities have the right to be educated in general education classrooms in their neighborhood schools with appropriate services, supplementary aids, and supports. Alternative placements should be rare and considered only when education in the general education classroom cannot be satisfactorily achieved. In order to provide a free, appropriate public education for students with I/DD, all those involved in the education of students with I/DD must:

- Fulfill the federal commitment to fund IDEA at 40%.
- Increase active monitoring and enforcement through local, state, and federal agencies to ensure that IDEA and state special education laws and mandates are met.
- Ensure that students with I/DD are educated to the maximum extent appropriate alongside students who do not have disabilities.
- Ensure that teachers and related services personnel, as well as their representatives, are prepared to teach and/or support students effectively in the general education curriculum and in inclusive settings.
- Serve students in the least restrictive environment (LRE), as determined for each student. Unless the Individualized Education Program (IEP) requires otherwise, the student attends the school s/he would have attended if s/he did not have a disability.
- Develop and implement IEPs that build on student strengths, meet the student's needs, and offer supports and services necessary to achieve success.
- Reflect sensitivity to linguistic, cultural, and socioeconomic diversity as well as diverse family circumstances.
- Provide access to the general education curriculum along with supplemental aids and services and extracurricular activities with same-age peers without disabilities.

- Foster the development of peer relationships and membership in the school community to create a receptive, welcoming atmosphere.
- Utilize the principles of Universal Design for Learning (UDL)[2] in designing curricula, materials, instruction, and assessments to create maximum access to learning environments for students with diverse abilities and learning styles.
- Incorporate evidence-based, peer-reviewed instructional strategies and interventions, provided by professionally qualified teachers, related services personnel, and other staff, all of whom receive the support they need.
- Ensure the meaningful involvement of students, families, their chosen advisors, and guardians in designing and monitoring the educational process at all levels.
- Connect students, families, and guardians with resources and training that help them understand their rights, procedural safeguards, and dispute resolution options.
- Incorporate and support the development of self-advocacy and leadership skills.
- Ensure that students with disabilities are not subjected to unwarranted restraint or isolation or to aversives. Physical restraint which restricts airflow, including prone restraint, and mechanical restraint must be prohibited.
- Ensure that all students have access to assistive technology, positive behavioral interventions and supports, and effective communication systems.
- Develop adaptations for assessment and grading.
- Provide early intervention and preschool services to infants, toddlers, and preschool-age children with disabilities alongside their typical peers and provide transition planning for children as they move to kindergarten or first grade.
- Develop and implement transition plans based on student strengths, preferences, and interests to facilitate movement from school to adult life, including postsecondary and vocational education, employment, independent living, and community participation.

Adopted:

Congress of Delegates, The Arc of the United States, 2011

Source: http://www.thearc.org/who-we-are/position-statements/life-in-the
-community/education

---

[2] "UDL" is an educational approach to curriculum and instruction using technology to enable students with diverse learning needs to be successful in the classroom. UDL means designing instructional methods and materials so individuals with differences in their abilities can achieve their learning goals.

Appendix G

The ARC Position Statement on Employment

The following position statement on employment was written by The Arc (http://www.thearc.org) and approved by the organization in 2012.

EMPLOYMENT

People with intellectual and/or developmental disabilities[1] can be employed in the community alongside people without disabilities and earn competitive wages. They should be supported to make informed choices about their work and careers and have the resources to seek, obtain, and be successful in community employment.

Issue

Historically, the majority of people with I/DD have been either unemployed or underemployed despite their ability, desire, and willingness to work in the community. Many have been placed in "prevocational" programs and "disability-only" workshops where they are paid below minimum wage and have little expectation of moving into jobs where they work alongside people without disabilities.

People often leave school with little community-based vocational experience or planning for transition from school to work or post-secondary education. Adult service agencies have struggled to move people into the workforce using personnel who often do not have proper training in best practices for either finding or supporting people in jobs. When employed, few people have opportunities to advance, explore new possibilities, or, in their later years, retire.

---

[1] "People with intellectual and/or developmental disabilities" [I/DD] refers to those defined by AAIDD classification and *DSM–IV*. In everyday language they are frequently referred to as people with cognitive, intellectual and/or developmental disabilities although the professional and legal definitions of those terms both include others and exclude some defined by *DSM*.

Barriers to employment include, first and foremost, low societal expectations that foster job discrimination. In addition, unrealistically low limits on assets and earnings make people fear losing vital public benefits if they work too many hours or earn too much. Systemically, public resources fund service hours rather than outcomes and are often neither sufficient nor flexible enough to allow collaboration and blending of employment funding streams. Lack of other services like transportation or of accommodations like assistive technology can also hinder success.

Position

People with I/DD should have the supports necessary from individuals and systems to enable them to find and keep community jobs based on their preferences, interests, and strengths, work alongside people without disabilities, receive comparable wages, and be free from workplace discrimination. Requirements related to employment include:

- Opportunities for post-secondary education, including college and vocational training, to gain knowledge and skills to allow people to get better jobs.
- Ongoing planning to promote job advancement and career development.
- Fair and reasonable wages and benefits.
- Opportunities for self-employment and business ownership.
- Opportunities to work with and, in the case of people with I/DD who own small businesses, employ people without disabilities.
- The ability to explore new directions over time and, at the appropriate time, retire.
- Opportunities to work and increase earnings and assets without losing eligibility for needed public benefits.

Best Practices

- Employment supports and services should use best practices, including assessing skills and interests, working with employers, matching jobs to skill sets and employer needs, providing individualized and ongoing job supports, designing reasonable job accommodations, integrating people into the workforce, building social skills necessary in the workplace, and securing necessary ancillary services such as transportation.
- People with I/DD must have training and information on how to access supports needed to find and keep jobs.

School-to-Work Transition

- Transition planning should start early.
- Transition activities should foster individualized exploration of and experiences with community-based employment options that enable youth to make informed choices.
- Transition activities should include career assessments to identify students' interests and preferences, exposure to post-secondary education and career opportunities, training to develop job-seeking and workplace skills, and participation in multiple on-the-job activities and experiences in paid and unpaid settings. Transition activities should not be limited to unpaid internships at pre-set community worksites.
- Students should leave high school with opportunities to pursue post-secondary education and/or with an appropriate job or an action plan for finding one.

Training of Staff and People with I/DD

- Staff of employment and school-to-work transition programs must receive training in best practices to help people find and keep jobs.
- Along with ensuring appropriate on-the-job training, people with I/DD should receive guidance, if needed, in acquiring the social skills necessary in the workplace.
- People with I/DD must have training, including, if desired, driver's education, to allow them to travel in the community so they can get to jobs and enhance their independence.

Systems

For all people with I/DD, publicly funded employment programs should first explore employment alongside people without disabilities at comparable wages, with comparable benefits, before considering other options in the community. Ancillary services like transportation and accommodations like assistive technology must be available to individuals and support agencies. Public policy should encourage employers to hire people with I/DD.

Publicly funded employment programs should also:

- Be available to all people with I/DD who wish to explore opportunities to work, regardless of the nature and extent of their disabilities.
- Enable people to make informed choices by providing individualized exploration of and experiences with community-based employment and

by presenting all information needed to make informed choices in an understandable way.

- Provide sufficient resources to support people to work in the community and be flexible enough to foster collaboration and braiding of employment-related funds.
- Build infrastructure and supports needed to phase out the issuance of subminimum wage certificates, increase opportunities for competitive integrated employment, and put in place safeguards to protect the interests of any people affected by this shift.
- Measure and publicly report on outcomes on an ongoing basis.

Adopted:

Board of Directors, The Arc
July 29, 2012

Congress of Delegates, The Arc
October 27, 2012

Source: http://www.thearc.org/who-we-are/position-statements/life-in-the
-community/employment

Appendix H

Helpful Websites

Alan W. Brue, Ph.D., NCSP

http://www.alanbrue.com

American Association on Intellectual and Developmental Disabilities (AAIDD)

444 North Capitol Street, NW, Suite 846
Washington, DC 20001
800-424-3688

http://www.aaidd.org

American Brain Tumor Association (ABTA)

2720 River Road
Des Plaines, IL 60018
800-886-2282

http://www.abta.org

American Physical Therapy Association (APTA)

1111 North Fairfax Street
Alexandria, VA 22314
800-999-2782

http://www.apta.org

American Occupational Therapy Association (AOTA)

4720 Montgomery Lane
P.O. Box 31220
Bethesda, MD 20824
301-652-2682

http://www.aota.org

American Speech-Language-Hearing-Association (ASHA)

2200 Research Boulevard
Rockville, MD 20850
800-638-8255

http://www.asha.org

Association on Higher Education and Disability (AHEAD)

107 Commerce Center Drive, Suite 204
Huntersville, NC 28078
704-947-7779

http://www.ahead.org

Autism Society (AS)

7910 Woodmont Avenue, Suite 300
Bethesda, MD 20814
800- 328-8476

http://www.autism-society.org

Brain Injury Association of America

1608 Spring Hill Road, Suite 110
Vienna, VA 22182
703-761-0750

http://www.biausa.org

Children's Tumor Foundation (CTF)

95 Pine Street, 16th Floor
New York, NY 10005
800-323-7938

http://www.ctf.org

Council for Exceptional Children (CEC)

1110 North Glebe Road, Suite 300
Arlington, VA 22201-5704
888-232-7733

http://www.cec.sped.org

Epilepsy Foundation

8301 Professional Place
Landover, MD 20785
800-332-1000

http://www.epilepsyfoundation.org

March of Dimes

1275 Mamaroneck Avenue
White Plains, NY 10605
914- 997-4488

http://www.marchofdimes.org

National Association of School Psychologists (NASP)

4340 East-West Highway, Suite 402
Bethesda, MD 20814
866-331-6277

http://www.nasponline.org

National Brain Tumor Foundation (NBTF)

22 Battery Street, Suite 612
San Francisco, CA 94111
800- 770 8287

http://www.braintumor.org

National Down Syndrome Society (NDSS)

666 Broadway, 8th Floor
New York, NY 10012
800-221-4602

http://www.ndss.org

National Fragile X Foundation

P.O. Box 190488
San Francisco, CA
800-688-8765

http://www.fragilex.org

National Organization on Fetal Alcohol Syndrome (NOFAS)

900 17th Street, NW, Suite 910
Washington, DC 20006
800-666-6327

http://www.nofas.org

Office of Special Education Programs (OSEP)

Office of Special Education and Rehabilitative Services
U.S. Department of Education
400 Maryland Avenue, SW
Washington, DC 20202
202-205-5507

http://www.ed.gov/about/offices/list/osers/osep/index.html

Prader-Willi Syndrome Association (PWSA)

8588 Potter Park Drive, Suite 500
Sarasota, FL 34238
800-926-4797

http://www.pwsausa.org

Special Olympics

1133 19th Street, N.W.
Washington, DC 20036
800-700-8585

http://www.specialolympics.org

Williams Syndrome Association (WSA)

570 Kirts Boulevard, Suite 223
Troy, MI 48084
800-806-1871

http://www.williams-syndrome.org

References

American Association on Intellectual and Developmental Disabilities. (AAIDD; 2010). *Intellectual disability: Definition, classification, and systems of support* (11th ed.). Washington, DC: Author.

American Psychiatric Association. (1952). *The diagnostic and statistical manual of mental disorders*. Washington, DC: Author.

American Psychiatric Association. (1968). *The diagnostic and statistical manual of mental disorders* (2nd ed.). Washington, DC: Author.

American Psychiatric Association. (1980). *The diagnostic and statistical manual of mental disorders* (3rd ed.). Washington, DC: Author.

American Psychiatric Association. (1994). *The diagnostic and statistical manual of mental disorders* (4th ed.). Washington, DC: Author.

American Psychiatric Association . (2000). *The diagnostic and statistical manual of mental disorders* (4th ed., text revision). Washington, DC: Author.

American Psychiatric Association. (2013). *The diagnostic and statistical manual of mental disorders* (5th ed.). Washington, DC: Author.

Anase, J. M., Jones, K. L., & Clarren, S. K. (1996), Do we need the term "FAE"? *Pediatrics, 95*, 428–430.

Bellugi, U., Jarvinen-Pasley, A., Doyle, T., Reilly, J., Reiss, A., & Korenberg, J. (2007). Affect, social behavior and the brain in Williams syndrome. *Current Directions in Psychological Science, 10*, 99–10.

Behnke, M., Smith, V. C., Levy, S., Ammerman, S. D., Gonzalez, P. K., Ryan, S. A., . . . & Watterberg, K. L. (2013). Prenatal substance abuse: short- and long-term effects on the exposed fetus. *Pediatrics, 131*(3), e1009-e1024.

Bergeron, R., Floyd, R., & Shands, E. I. (2008). States' eligibility criterion for mental retardation: An update, and consideration of part scores and unreliability of IQs. *Education and Training in Developmental Disabilities, 43*(1), 123–131.

Biasini, F., Grupe, L., Juffman, L., & Bray, N. W. (1999). Mental retardation: A symptom and a syndrome. In S. D. Netherton, D. Holmes, & E. C. Walker (Eds.), *Child and adolescent psychological disorders: A comprehensive textbook* (pp. 6–23). New York, NY: Oxford University Press.

Blatt, B., & Kaplan, F. (1966). *Christmas in purgatory: A photographic essay on mental retardation*. Boston, MA: Allyn & Bacon.

Blume, J. H., & Salekin, K. L. (2015). Analysis of Atkins cases. In E. A. Polloway (Ed.), *The death penalty and intellectual disability*. Washington, DC: American Association on Intellectual and Developmental Disabilities.

Bronfenbrenner, U. (1989). Ecological systems theory. *Annals of Child Development, 6*, 187–249.

Brown, C., Goodman, S., & Kupper, L. (2003). The unplanned journey. *New Digest, 20* (3rd ed.), pp. 7–16: Washington, DC: NICHCY.

Brown, W., Jenkins, E., Cohen, I., Fisch, G., Wolf-Schein, E., & Waterhouse, L. (1986). Fragile X and autism: A multicenter survey. *American Journal of Medical Genetics, 23*, 341–350.

Calkins, C. F., Jackson, L. W., & Beckmann, C. (2011). Self-determination and self-advocacy. In *Research to practice in self-determination* (pp. 3–5). Retrieved from http://ngsd.org/sites/default/files/research_to_practice_sd_-_issue_1_0.pdf

Canfield, R. L., Henderson, C. R., Cory-Slechta, D. A., Cox, C., Jusko, T. A., & Lanphear, B. P. (2003). Intellectual impairment in children with blood lead concentrations below 10 µg per deciliter. *New England Journal of Medicine, 348*, 1517–1526.

Carlson, J. F., Geisinger, K. F., & Jonson, J. L. (Eds.). (2014). *Mental measurements yearbook* (19th ed.). Lincoln, NE: Buros Center for Testing.

Carvill, S., & Marston, G. (2002). People with intellectual disability, sensory impairments and behavior disorder: A case series. *Journal of Intellectual Disability Research, 26*, 264–272.

Cassidy, S. B., & Driscoll, D. J. (2009). Prader-Willi syndrome. *European Journal of Human Genetics, 17*, 3-13.

Cernerud, L. A. R. S., Eriksson, M., Jonsson, B., Steneroth, G., & Zetterstrom, R. (1996). Amphetamine addiction during pregnancy: 14-year follow-up of growth and school performance. *Acta paediatrica, 85*(2), 204-208.

Chaste, P., Betancur, C., Gerard-Blanluet, M., Bargiacchi, A., Kuzbari, S., Drunat, S.,... Delorme, R. (2012). High functioning autism spectrum disorder and fragile X syndrome: Report of the two affected sisters. *Molecular Autism, 3*(1), 5.

Clayton-Smith, J. (1993). Clinical research on Angelman syndrome in the United Kingdom: Observations on 82 affected individuals. *American Journal of Medical Genetics, 993*, 12–15.

Clayton-Smith, J., & Laan, L. (2003). Angelman syndrome: A review of the clinical and genetic aspects. *Journal of Medical Genetics, 40*, 87–95.

Clickner, R. P., Zhou, J., Viet, S. M., Marker, D., Rogers, J. W., Zeldin, D. C., Broene, P., & Friedman, W. (2002). The prevalence of lead-based paint hazards in U.S. housing. *Environmental Health Perspectives, 110*(10), 599–606.

Clifford, S., Dissananyake, C., Bui, Q., Huggins, R., Taylor, A., & Loesch, D. (2007). Autism spectrum phenotype in males and females with fragile X full mutation and permutation. *Journal of Autism and Developmental Disorders, 37*(4), 738–747.

Close, D. W., & Walker, H. M. (2010). Navigating the criminal justice system for youth and adults with developmental disabilities: Role of the forensic special educator. *Journal of Behavior Analysis of Offender & Victim: Treatment & Planning, 2*(2), 74–102.

Colon, R., Lluis-Font, J. M., & Andres-Pueyo, A. (2005). The generational intelligence gains are caused by decreasing variance in the lower half of the distribution: Supporting evidence for the nutrition hypothesis. *Intelligence, 33*, 83–91.

Comer, R. J. (2010). *Abnormal psychology* (7th ed). New York, NY: Worth.

Committee on Environmental Health. (2005). Lead exposure in children: Prevention, detection, and management. *Pediatrics, 116*(4), 1036–11046.

Connor, P. D., Sampson, P., & Bookstein, F. L. (2001). Direct and indirect effects of prenatal alcohol damage on executive function. *Developmental Neuropsychology, 18*, 331–354.

Connor, P. D., Sampson, P. D., Bookstein, F. L., Barr, H. M., & Streissguth, A. P. (2000). Direct and indirect effects of prenatal alcohol damage on executive function. *Developmental Neuropsychology, 18*, 331–354.

Das, J. P., Kar, R., & Parrila, R. K. (1996). *Cognitive planning: The psychological basis of intelligent behavior*. London, UK: Sage.

Das, J. P., Kirby, J. R., & Jarman, R. F. (1975). Simultaneous and successive syntheses: An alternative model for cognitive abilities. *Psychological Bulletin, 82*, 87–103.

Das, J. P., Naglieri, J. A., & Kirby, J. R. (1994). *Assessment of cognitive processes: The PASS theory of intelligence*. Boston, MA: Allyn & Bacon.

Davis, D. W., Change, F., Burns, B., Robinson, J., & Dossett, D. (2004). Lead exposure and attention regulation in children living in poverty. *Developmental Medicine & Child Neurology, 46*, 825–831.

Dekker, M. C., & Koot, H. M. (2003). *DSM–IV* disorders in children with borderline to moderate intellectual disability: Prevalence and impact. *Journal of the American Academy of Child & Adolescent Psychiatry, 42*, 915–922.

Denning, C. B., Chamberlain, J. A., & Polloway, E. A. (2000). An evaluation of state guidelines for mental retardation: Focus on definition and classification practices. *Education and Training in Mental Retardation and Developmental Disabilities, 35*, 226–232.

Donlon, J., Levy, H., & Scriver, C. R. (2004). Hyperphenylalaninemia: Phenylalanine hydroxylase deficiency. In C. R. Scriver, A. R. Beaudet, W. S. Sly, & D. Valle (Eds.), *The metabolic and molecular bases of inherited disease* (pp. 1821–1838). New York, NY: McGraw-Hill.

Duvall, J. C., & Morris, R. J. (2006). Assessing mental retardation in death penalty cases: Critical issues for psychology and psychological practice. *Professional Psychology: Research and Practice, 37*(6), 658–665).

Dykens, E. M., & Cassidy, S. B. (1995). Correlates of maladaptive behavior in children and adults with Prader-Willi syndrome. *Neuropsychiatric Genetics, 60*, 546–549.

Eberhart-Phillips, J. E., Frederick, P. D., Baron, R. C., & Mascola, L. (1993). Measles in pregnancy: A descriptive study of 58 cases. *Obstetrics and Gynecology, 82*(5), 797–801.

Ellis, J. W. (1992). Decisions by and for people with mental retardation: Balancing considerations of autonomy and protection. *Villanova Law Review, 37*, 1779–1809.

Ellis, J. W. (2013). The law's understanding of intellectual disability as a disability. *Intellectual and Developmental Disabilities, 51*(2), 102–107.

Emerson, E. (2003). Prevalence of psychiatric disorders in children and adolescents with and without intellectual disability. *Journal of Intellectual Disability Research, 47*, 51–58.

Epsy, K. A., Kaufmann, P. M., & Glisky, M. L. (1999). Neuropsychologic function in toddlers exposed to cocaine in utero: A preliminary study. *Developmental Neuropsychology, 15*, 447–460.

Everington, C., & Keyes, D. W. (1999). Diagnosing mental retardation in criminal proceedings: The critical importance of documenting adaptive behavior. *Forensic Examiner, 8*(7–8), 31–34.

Eversman, K. (2011). *Using Lifebooks for self-advocacy.* In Research to practice in self-determination (pp. 11–16). Retrieved from http://ngsd.org/sites/default/files/research_to_practice_sd_-_issue_1_0.pdf

Ferguson, D. L., Ferguson, P. M., & Wehmeyer, M. L. (2013) The self-advocacy movement. In M. L. Wehmeyer (Ed.)., *The story of intellectual disability: An evolution of meaning, understanding, & public perception* (pp. 233–277). Baltimore, MD: Paul Brookes.

Field, S., Martin, J., Miller, R., Ward, M., & Wehmeyer, M. (1998). *A practical guide to teaching self-determination.* Reston, VA: Council for Exceptional Children.

Fisch, H., Hyun, G., Golden, R., Hensle, T. W., Olsson, C. S., & Liberson, G. L. (2003). The influence of paternal age on Down syndrome. *Journal of Urology, 169*(6), 2275–2278.

Flanagan, D. P., McGrew, K. S., & Ortiz, S. O. (2000). *The Wechsler intelligence scales and CHC theory: A contemporary approach to interpretation.* Boston, MA: Allyn & Bacon.

Fletcher, J. M., Stuebing, K. K., & Hughes, L. C. (2010). IQ scores should be corrected for the Flynn effect in high-stakes decisions. *Journal of Psychoeducational Assessment, 28*(5), 469–473.

Flynn, J. R. (1984). The mean IQ of Americans: Massive gains 1932–1978. *Psychological Bulletin, 95*(1), 29–51.

Flynn, J. R. (2012). *Are we getting smarter? Rising IQ in the twenty-first century*. New York, NY: Cambridge University Press.

Ford, M., Acosta, A., & Sutcliffe, T. J. (2013). Beyond terminology: The policy impact of a grassroots movement. *Intellectual and Developmental Disabilities, 51*(2), 108–112.

Fowler, A. (1990). Language abilities in children with Down syndrome: Evidence for a specific syntactic delay. In D. Cicchetti & M. Beeghly (Eds.), *Children with Down syndrome: A developmental perspective* (pp. 302–328). Cambridge, UK: Cambridge University Press.

Freeman, S. B., Taft, L. F., Dooley, K. J., Allran, K., Sherman, S. L., Hassold, T. J., . . . Saker, D. M. (1998). Population-based study of congenital heart defects in Down syndrome. *American Journal of Medical Genetics, 80*(3), 213–217.

Freund, L., Reiss, A., & Abrams, M. (1993). Psychiatric disorders associated with fragile X in the young female. *Pediatrics, 91*(2), 321–329.

Gardner, H. (1983). *Frames of mind: The theory of multiple intelligences*. New York, NY: Basic Books.

Gardner, H. (1999). Are there additional intelligences? In J. Kane (Ed.), *Education, information and transformation* (pp. 111–131). Upper Saddle River, NJ: Prentice Hall.

Gardner, H., & Moran, S. (2006). The science of multiple intelligences theory: A response to Lynn Waterhouse. *Educational Psychologist, 41*(4), 227–232.

Grant, S. (2006). Down syndrome demystified. *Pediatrics for Parents, 22*(4), 5–11.

Gresham, F. M. (2009). Interpretation of intelligence test scores in *Atkins* cases: Conceptual and psychometric issues. *Applied Neuropsychology, 16*, 91–97.

Grossman, H. J. (Ed.). (1973). *Manual on the terminology in mental retardation* (Rev. ed.). Washington, DC: American Association on Mental Deficiency.

Hagan, L. D., Drogin, E. Y., & Guilmette, T. J. (2010). IQ scores should not be adjusted for the Flynn effect in capital punishment cases. *Journal of Psychoeducational Assessment, 28*(5), 469–473.

Hagerman, R. J. (2002). The physical and behavioral phenotype. In R. J. Hagerman & P. J. Hagerman (Eds.), *Fragile X syndrome: Diagnosis, treatment and research* (3rd ed.) (pp. 3–109). Baltimore, MD: John Hopkins University Press.

Hall, S., De Bernardis, M., & Reiss, A. (2006). Social escape behaviors in children with fragile X syndrome. *Journal of Autism and Developmental Disorders, 36*, 935–947.

Hardelid, P., Cortina-Borja, M., Munro, A., Jones, H., Clearly, M., Champion, M.P., . . . Dezateux, C. (2008). The birth prevalence of PKU in populations of European, South Asian and Sub-Saharan African ancestry living in south east England. *Annals of Human Genetics, 72*(1), 65–71.

Horn, J. L., & Cattell, R. B. (1966). Refinement and test of the theory of fluid and crystallized general intelligences. *Journal of Educational Psychology, 57*(5), 253–270.

Horsler, K., & Oliver, C. (2006). The behavioral phenotype of Angelman syndrome. *Journal of Intellectual Disability Research, 50*, 33–53.

Hoyme, H. D., May, P. A., Kalberg, W. O., Kodituwakku, P., Gossage, P., & Trujillo, P. (2005). A practical clinical approach to diagnosis of fetal alcohol spectrum disorders: Clarification of the 1996 Institute of Medicine criteria. *Pediatrics, 115*, 39–47.

Hunley, S. (2011) *Assisted technology that is affordable*. In Research to Practice in Self-Determination (pp. 12–16). Retrieved from http://ngsd.org/sites/default/files/research_to_practice_sd_-_issue_1_0.pdf

Kassin, S. (2005). On the psychology of confessing. *American Psychologist, 60*(3), 215–228.

Kaufman, A. S., & Weiss, L. G. (2010). Guest editors' introductions to the special issue of JPA on the Flynn effect. *Journal of Psychoeducational Assessment, 28*(5), 379–381.

Kaufman, J. C., Kaufman, S. B., & Plucker, J. A. (2013). Contemporary theories of intelligence. In D. Reisberg (Ed.), *The Oxford handbook of cognitive psychology* (pp. 811–822). New York, NY: Oxford University Press.

Kirk, S. A., Karnes, M. B., & Kirk, W. D. (1955). *You and your retarded child*. New York, NY: Macmillan.

Koury, M. J., Burke, W., & Thomson, E. (2000). Genetics and public health: A framework for the integration of human genetics into public health practice. In M. J. Koury, W. Burke, & E. Thomson (Eds.), *Genetics & public health in the 21st Century: Using genetic information to improve health and prevent disease* (pp. 3–25). New York, NY: Oxford University Press.

Kumin, L. (1994). Intelligibility of speech in children with Down syndrome in natural settings: Parent's perspective. *Perceptual and Motor Skills, 78*, 307–313.

Larry P. v. Riles, 343E Supp. 1306 (N.D. Cal. 1972), *aff'd 502* F 2d 963.

Leo, R. A., & Ofshe, R. J. (1998). The consequences of false confessions. *Journal of Criminal Law, and Criminology, 88*(2), 429–496.

Lester, B. M., LaGasse, L. L., & Seifer, R. (1998). Cocaine exposure and children: The meaning of subtle effects. *Science, 282*(5389), 633–634.

Liptak, A. (2014, May 27). *Court extends curbs on the death penalty in a Florida ruling. New York Times*. Retrieved from http://www.nytimes.com/2014/05/28/us/court-rules-against-florida-iq-rule-in-death-cases.html?_r=1

Little, B. B., Snell, L. M., Rosenfeld, C. R., Gilstrap, L. C., & Gant, N. F. (1990). Failure to recognize fetal alcohol syndrome in newborn infants. *American Journal of Disabilities in Children, 144*, 1142–1146.

Luckasson, R., Borthwick-Duffy, S., Buntinx, W. H. E., Coulter, D. L., Craig, E. M., Reeve, A., . . . Tasse, M. J. (2002). *Mental retardation: Definition, classification, and systems of supports* (10th ed.). Washington, DC: American Association on Mental Retardation.

Luckasson, R., Coulter, D. L., Polloway, E. A., Reiss, S., Schalock, R. L., Snell, M. E., . . . Stark, J. A. (1992). *Mental retardation: Definition, classification, and systems of supports* (9th ed.). Washington, DC: American Association on Mental Retardation.

Luria, A. R. (1966). *Human brain and psychological processes*. New York, NY: Harper & Row.

MacMillan, D. L., & Forness, S. R. (1998). The role of IQ in special education placement decisions: Primary and determinative or peripheral and inconsequential? *Remedial and Special Education, 19*, 239–253.

Malich, S., Largo, R. H., Schinzel, A., Molinari, L., & Eiholzer, U. (2000). Phenotypic heterogeneity of growth and psychometric intelligence in Prader-Willi syndrome: Variable expression of a contiguous gene syndrome or parent-child resemblance? *American Journal of Medical Genetics, 91*, 298–304.

Mayes, L. C., Granger, R. H., Bornstein, M. H., & Zuckerman, B. (1992). The problem of prenatal cocaine exposure: A rush to judgment. *JAMA, 267*(3), 406–408.

McGrew, K. S. (2010). The Flynn effect and its critics: Rusty linchpins and "lookin' for g and Gf in some of the wrong places." *Journal of Psychoeducational Assessment, 28*(5), 448–468.

McGrew, K. S. (2011). Time to stop executing the mentally retarded: The case of applying the standard errors of measurement. Retrieved from http://www.iapsych.com/iapap101/iapap10111.pdf

McGrew, K. S., & Flanagan, D. P. (1998). *The intelligence test desk reference (ITDR): Gf-Gc cross-battery assessment*. Boston, MA: Allyn & Bacon.

Merenstein, S., Shyu, V., Sobesky, W., Staley, L., Berry-Kravis, E., Nelson D., . . . Hagerman, R. (1994). Fragile X syndrome in a normal IQ male with learning and emotional problems. *Journal of the American Academy of Child & Adolescent Psychiatry, 33*(9), 1316–1321.

Meyer-Lindenberg, A., Hariri, A., Munoz, K., Mervin, C., Mattay, V., & Morris, C. A. (2005). Neural correlates of genetically abnormal social cognition in Williams syndrome. *Nature Neuroscience, 8*, 991–993.

Miller, J. F. (1999). Profiles of language development in children with Down syndrome. In J. F. Miller, M. Leddy, & L. A. Leavitt (Eds.), *Improving the communication of people with Down syndrome* (pp. 11–39). Baltimore, MD: Paul Brookes.

Milner, K. M., Craig, E. E., Thompson, R., Veltman, W. M., Thomas, N. S., & Roberts, S. (2005). Prader-Willi syndrome: Intellectual abilities and behavioral features by genetic subtype. *Journal of Child Psychology and Psychiatry, 46*, 1089–1096.

Morris, J.K., Mutton, D.E., & Alberman, E. (2002). Revised estimates of the maternal age specific live birth prevalence of Down's syndrome. *Journal of Medical Screening, 9*(1), 2–6.

Nanson, J. L., & Hiscock, M. (1990). Attention deficits in children exposed to alcohol prenatally. *Alcoholism: Clinical and Experimental Research, 14*(5), 656–661.

National Archives and Records Administration. (2005). Assistance to states for the education of children with disabilities, Federal Register, *70* (118). Washington DC: Government Printing Office

Nietzel, M., Bernstein, D., & Milich, R. (1994). *Introduction to clinical psychology* (4th ed). Englewood Cliffs, NJ: Prentice Hall.

Olley, J. G. (2013). Definition of intellectual disability in criminal court cases. *Intellectual and Developmental Disabilities, 51*(2), 117–121.

Palmer, L. J. (2008). *Encyclopedia of capital punishment in the United States* (2nd ed.). Jefferson, NC: McFarland.

Parrish, T. (2002). Racial disparities in the identification, funding, and provision of special education. In D. J. Losen & G. Orfield (Eds.), *Racial inequity in special education* (pp. 15–37). Cambridge, MA: Harvard Education Press.

Parry, J. (1997). *Mental disabilities and the Americans with Disabilities Act* (2nd ed.). Washington, DC: American Bar Association Commission on Mental and Physical Disability Law.

Pennington, B.R., Moon, J., Edgin, J., Stedron, J., & Nadel, L. (2003). The neuropsychology of Down syndrome: Evidence for hippocampal dysfunction. *Child Development, 74*(1), 75– 93.

Perkins, J. A. (2009). Overview of macroglossia and its treatment. *Current Opinion in Otolaryngology & Head and Neck Surgery, 17*(6), 460–465.

Pocock, S. J., Smith, M., & Baghurst, P. (1994). Environmental lead and children's intelligence: A systematic review of the epidemiological evidence. *British Medical Journal, 309*(6963), 1189–1197.

Reiss, A. L., & Dant, C .C. (2003). The behavioral neurogenetics of fragile X syndrome: Analyzing gene–brain–behavior relationships in child developmental psychopathologies. *Development and Psychopathology, 4*, 927–968.

Reschly, D. J., Myers, T. G., & Hartel, C. R. (Eds.). (2002). *Mental retardation: Determining eligibility for social security benefits*. Washington, DC: National Academy Press.

Resta, R. (2012). Generation n + 1: Projected numbers of babies born to women with PKU compared to babies with PKU in the United States in 2009. *American Journal of Medical Genetics, 158A*(5), 1118–1123.

Richardson, G. A., Conroy, M. L., & Day, N. L. (1996). Prenatal cocaine exposure: Effects on the development of school-age children. *Neurotoxicology and Teratology, 18*(6), 627–634.

Richardson, G. A., Hamel, S. C., & Goldschmidt, L. (1996). The effects of prenatal cocaine use on neonatal neurobehavioral status. *Neurotoxicology and Teratology, 18*, 519–528.

Rogers, J. L., & Wanstrom, L. (2007). Identification of a Flynn effect in the NLSY: Moving from the center to the boundaries. *Intelligence, 35*, 187–196.

Roizen, N. J., Walters, C. A., Nicol, T. G., & Blondis, T. A. (1993). Auditory brainstem evoked response in children with Down syndrome. *Journal of Pediatrics, 123*(1), S9–12.

Roubertou, P. L., & Kerdelhue, B. (2006). Trisomy 21: From chromosomes to mental retardation. *Behavior Genetics, 36*, 346–354.

Rourke, B. P., Ahmad, S., Collins, D., Jayman-Abello, B., Hayman-Abello, S., & Warriner, E. M. (2002). Child clinical/pediatric neuropsychology: Some recent advances. *Annual Review of Psychology, 53*, 309–339.

Sattler, J. M. (2001). *Assessment of children: Cognitive applications* (2nd ed.). San Diego, CA: Author.

Schalock, R. (2012). *Classification and intellectual disability.* Retrieved from http://www.youtube.com/watch?v=80rc4ZAtQ0I

Schalock, R. L., Shogren, K. A., Luckasson, R., Borthwick-Duffy, S., Buntinx, W. H. E., Coulter, D., . . . Yeager, M. (2007). The renaming of mental retardation: Understanding the change to the term intellectual disability. *Intellectual and Developmental Disabilities, 45*, 116–124.

Schlinger, H. D. (2003). The myth of intelligence. *Psychological Record, 53*, 15–32.

Schonfeld, A., Mattson, S. N., & Lang, A. (2001). Verbal and nonverbal fluency in children with heavy prenatal alcohol exposure. *Journal of Studies on Alcohol, 62*, 239–246.

Schweinhart, L. J., & Fulcher-Dawson, R. (2009). Early childhood education. In G. Sykes, B. Schneider, & D. N. Plank (Eds.), *Handbook of education policy research* (pp. 876–888). New York, NY: Routledge.

Schweinhart, L. J., Montie, J., Xiang, Z., Barnett, W. S., Belfield, C. R., & Nores, M. (2005). *Lifetime effects: The HighScope Perry Preschool study through age 40.* (Monographs of the HighScope Educational Research Foundation, 14). Ypsilanti, MI: HighScope Press.

Shannon, S. A. G. (2003). *Atkins v. Virginia*: Commutation for the mentally retarded? *South Carolina Law Review, 54*, 809–1131.

Sheerenberger, R. C. (1983). *A history of mental retardation.* Baltimore, MD: Paul Brookes.

Shogren, K. (2013). A social-ecological analysis of the self-determination literature. *Intellectual and Developmental Disabilities, 51*(6), 496–511.

Shogren, K. A., Wehmeyer, M. L., Palmer, S. B., Soukup, J. H., Little, T. D., Garner, N., & Lawrence, M. (2007). Examining individual and ecological predictors of the self-determination of students with disabilities. *Exceptional Children, 73*, 488–509.

Skiba, R. J., Simmons, A. B., Ritter, S., Gibb, A. C., Rausch, M. K., Cuadrado, J., & Chung, C. (2008). Achieving equity in special education: History, status, and current challenges. *Exceptional Children, 74*(3), 264–288.

Smith, A., & Kozleski, E. B. (2005). Witnessing Brown. *Remedial and Special Education, 26*(5), 270–280.

Smith, P. M. (2003). You are not alone. *New Digest, 20* (3rd ed.), pp. 2–6: Washington, DC: NICHCY.

Spearman, C. (1904). "General intelligence," objectively determined and measured. *American Journal of Psychology 15*, 201–293.

Steen, R. G. (2009). *Human intelligence and medical illness: Assessing the Flynn effect.* New York, NY: Springer.

Sternberg, R. J. (1985). *Beyond IQ: A triarchic theory of intelligence.* New York, NY: Cambridge University Press.

Sternberg, R. J. (2010). The Flynn effect: So what? *Journal of Psychoeducational Assessment, 28*(5), 434–440.

Streissguth, A. P., Bookstein, F. L., & Barr, H. M. (2004). Risk factors for adverse life outcomes in fetal alcohol syndrome and fetal alcohol effects. *Journal of Developmental & Behavioral Pediatrics, 25*, 228–238.

Streissguth, A. P., Bookstein, P. I., Barr, H. M., Sampson, P., O'Mally, K., & Young, J. K. (2004). Risk factors for adverse life outcomes in fetal alcohol syndrome and fetal alcohol effects. *Developmental and Behavioral Pediatrics, 25*, 226–238.

Substance Abuse and Mental Health Services Administration. (2007). *Fetal alcohol spectrum disorders and juvenile justice: How professionals can make a difference.* Retrieved from http://www.fasdcenter.samhsa.gov/documents/WYNK_JuvJust_Profs.pdf

Taylor, J., & Krauss, D. (2014). Revisiting intellectual disability and the death penalty. *Monitor on Psychology, 45*(4), 26.

Teasdale, T. W., & Owen D. R. (2005). A long-term rise and recent decline in intelligence test performance: The Flynn effect in reverse. *Personality and Individual Differences, 39*, 837–843.

Thatcher, R., Lyon, G., Rumsey, J., & Krasnegor, J. (1996). *Developmental neuroimaging.* San Diego, CA: Academic Press.

Thompson, J., Hughes, C., Schalock, R., Silverman, W., Tassé, M. J., & Bryant, B. (2002). Integrating supports into assessment and planning. *Mental Retardation, 40*, 390–405.

Thompson, J. R., Bryant, B., Campbell, E. M., Craig, E. M., Hughes, C., Rotholz, D., . . . Wehmeyer, M. L. (2004). *Supports Intensity Scale: Standardization and users manual.* Washington, DC: American Association on Mental Retardation.

Thurstone, L. L. (1938). Primary mental abilities. *Psychometric Monographs, 1*, ix–121.

Turner, G., Webb, T., Wake, S., & Robinson, H. (1996). Prevalence of fragile X syndrome. *American Journal of Medical Genetics, 64*, 196–197.

Tylenda, B., & Brogan, D. T. (2011). More than numbers: Intelligence testing with the intellectually disabled. *Brown University Child and Adolescent Behavior Letter, 27*(10), 1, 5.

Vicari, S. (2005). Motor development and neuropsychological patterns in persons with Down syndrome. *Behavior Genetics, 36*, 355–364.

Ward, M. J. (1996). Coming of age in the age of self-determination. A historical and personal perspective. In D. J. Sands & M. L. Wehmeyer (Eds.), *Self-determination across the lifespan: Independence and choice for people with disabilities* (pp. 1–14). Baltimore, MD: Paul Brookes.

Warlick, S. E., & Dougherty, R. V. P. (2015). *Hall v. Florida* reinvigorates concept of protection for intellectually disabled. *Criminal Justice, 29*(4), 4–8.

Wechsler, D. (1949). *Wechsler Intelligence Scale for Children.* New York, NY: The Psychological Corporation.

Wechsler, D. (1974). *Wechsler Intelligence Scale for Children—Revised Edition.* San Antonio, TX: The Psychological Corporation.

Wechsler, D. (1991). *Wechsler Intelligence Scale for Children—Third Edition.* San Antonio, TX: The Psychological Corporation.

Wechsler, D. (2003). *Wechsler Intelligence Scale for Children—Fourth Edition.* San Antonio, TX: Harcourt.

Wechsler, D. (2014). *Wechsler Intelligence Scale for Children—Fifth Edition.* San Antonio, TX: Pearson.

Wehmeyer, M. L., Chapman, T. E., Little, T. D., Thompson, J. R., Schalock, R., & Tasse M. J. (2009). Efficacy of the Supports Intensity Scale (SIS) to predict extraordinary support needs. *American Journal on Intellectual and Developmental Disabilities, 114*(1), 3–14.

Wehmeyer, M. L., & Schalock, L (2013). The parent movement. In M. L Wehmeyer (Ed.)., *The story of intellectual disability: An evolution of meaning, understanding, & public perception* (pp. 187–231). Baltimore, MD: Paul Brookes.

Wehmeyer, M. L., Tasse, M. J., Davies, D. K., & Stock, S. (2012). Support needs of adults with intellectual disability across domains: The role of technology. *Journal of Special Education Technology, 27*(2), 11–21.

Weijerman, M. E., & de Winter, J. P (2010). Clinical practice. The care of children with Down syndrome. *European Journal of Pediatrics 169*(12), 1445–1452.

Wickman, P. (2013). Idiocy and early modern law: Intellectual disability in early modern times (1500 CE to 1799 CE). In M. L Wehmeyer (Ed.), *The story of intellectual disability: An evolution of meaning, understanding, & public perception* (pp. 63–78). Baltimore, MD: Paul Brookes.

Wigren, M., & Hansen, S. (2005). ADHD symptoms and insistence on sameness in Prader-Willi syndrome. *Journal of Intellectual Disability Research, 49,* 449–456.

Wilmshurst, L., & Brue, A. W. (2010). *The complete guide to special education: Expert advice on evaluations, IEPs, and helping kids succeed* (2nd ed). San Francisco, CA: Jossey Bass.

World Health Organization (WHO; 1992). *The ICD-10 Classification of Mental and Behavioral Disorders, Clinical Descriptions and Diagnostic Guidelines.* Geneva, Switzerland: WHO.

Wouldes, T., LaGasse, L., Sheridan, J., & Lester, B. (2004). Maternal methamphetamine use during pregnancy and child outcome: what do we know. *New Zealand Medical Journal, 117*(1206), 1–10.

Zenderland, L. (2004). The parable of the Kallikak family: Explaining the meaning of heredity in 1912. In S. Noll & J. Trent (Eds.). *Mental retardation in America: A historical reader* (pp. 165–185). New York, NY: New York University Press.

Zhou, X., Zhu, J., & Weiss, L. G. (2010). Peeking inside the "black box" of the Flynn effect: Evidence from three Wechsler instruments. *Journal of Psychoeducational Assessment, 28*(5), 399–411.

About the Authors

Alan W. Brue, Ph.D., NCSP, received his master's, specialist, and doctoral degrees in school psychology from the University of Florida. Alan is a nationally certified school psychologist who has worked for many years providing a wide range of school psychological services to metro-Atlanta school districts. In addition to his school-based experience, Alan also holds a core faculty teaching position in a school psychology training program, where he teaches classes such as Psychological Assessment, Exceptional Children in the Classroom, Psychopathology of Children and Adolescents, Tests and Measurements, Child and Adolescent Psychology, and Lifespan Development. He has been a co-principal investigator, site coordinator, examiner, and/or reviewer for more than 20 assessment measures (cognitive, achievement, behavior, adaptive behavior, and speech-language). When he was a doctoral student, Alan was hired by his advisor, Thomas Oakland, to write test items for the original Adaptive Behavior Assessment System (ABAS), which was created by Drs. Patti Harrison and Thomas Oakland and currently is one of the leading adaptive behavior measures. With Linda Wilmshurst, he has coauthored *The Complete Guide to Special Education: Expert Advice on Evaluations, IEPs, and Helping Kids Succeed (Second Edition)* (Jossey-Bass, 2010) and *A Parent's Guide to Special Education: Insider Advice on How to Navigate the System and Help Your Child Succeed* (AMACOM, 2005). With Stephanie M. Hadaway, he has coauthored *Practitioner's Guide to Functional Behavioral Assessment: Process, Purpose, Planning, and Prevention* (Springer, 2016).

Linda Wilmshurst, Ph.D., ABPP, received her doctorate from the University of Toronto and has had extensive international involvement with children, adolescents, and their families in private practice, academic, clinical, and school settings. She is a Diplomate in Clinical Psychology and is a licensed psychologist and licensed school psychologist in Florida. Linda has held academic positions in the psychology departments at Texas Woman's University; the University of Houston, Victoria; the University of Western Ontario; and Elon University in North Carolina, where she was an associate professor for nine years prior to relocating to Florida. Currently Linda provides clinical services for children, adolescents and their families at the Center for Psychology in Florida and she continues to teach graduate courses for Capella University. She has authored several books: *Essentials of Child and Adolescent Psychopathology* (Wiley, 2015), *Child and Adolescent Psychopathology: A Casebook (Third Edition)* (Sage, 2014); *Clinical and Educational Child Psychology: An Ecological-Transactional Approach to Understanding Child Problems and Interventions* (Wiley, 2013); and *Abnormal Child Psychology: A Developmental Perspective* (Rutledge, 2009). In addition, with Alan Brue, she has coauthored *The Complete Guide to Special Education: Expert Advice on Evaluations, IEPs, and Helping Kids Succeed (Second Edition)* (Jossey-Bass, 2010) and *A Parent's Guide to Special Education: Insider Advice on How to Navigate the System and Help Your Child Succeed* (AMACOM, 2005).

Index